manage-
ment
plus

manage-ment plus

Getting Things
Done
Through People

by Richard LeTourneau

ZONDERVAN PUBLISHING HOUSE OF THE ZONDERVAN CORPORATION GRAND RAPIDS, MICHIGAN 49506

MANAGEMENT "PLUS"
© 1973 by The Zondervan Corporation
Grand Rapids, Michigan

Library of Congress Catalog Card Number 73-8361

Fifth printing (First Zondervan Books Edition) 1976

Printed in the United States of America

CONTENTS

The ability to relate to people and their
needs in such a way that even a tough
and exacting manner will be recognized
as fair and empathetic.

PART THREE: PRINCIPLE RELATED QUALITIES

The ability to accept responsibility and
shoulder it squarely without passing the buck
when it falls into your realm whether
or not you could have controlled it.

A reputation for fulfillment of all promises
as well as a stability of character that
inspires confidence.

The ability to maintain a stance and a
calmness even in periods of flexibility and
change, that inspires confidence and
security in your team.

PART FOUR: PERSONALITY RELATED QUALITIES

The possession of a contagious enthusiasm
for the job, the product, or service of the
company and the people who produce it.

The ability to react, or refrain from reacting,
to situations, and a sensitivity to the need
for action rather than reaction or passivity.

The ability to recover from mistakes or
misfortunes (of yourself or others) with
sufficient rapidity so as not to compound
errors by dwelling on the past.

PART SEVEN: SPECIAL "PLUS" QUALITIES

PREFACE

This book is unique in the field of management literature in that it adds a "plus" element to the generally accepted characteristics and requirements of good management. Over the years I have accumulated a large number of books dealing with the various facets of management, executive behavior, organizational philosophy and people relationships. These books cover a wide range of approaches to the particular problem of managing people in various types of organizations and businesses. Some approach situations from the manager's side and some approach them from the employee's side. Some are serious college textbooks, others are written strictly for the lay reader. Some even immerse the basic facets and truths of management and organization in a humorous vein. I have particularly enjoyed reading these witty books because generally behind the humor lies some very solid management truths that become all the more striking when placed in a relaxed and entertaining framework.

In all of these books, however, whether they be comprehensive college text books or informal best sellers, I have searched in vain for the *one* segment of management philosophy and capabilities that my own experiences have shown to be vitally necessary and usually present in almost every really successful management situation. This quality seems to be so elusive that authors have either ignored or avoided it. Since it is difficult to define, it is also difficult for the average executive or textbook author to pinpoint. It involves that extra something, that extra sense, that extra bit of intuition or guidance in making decisions and handling people that often makes the difference between success and failure.

Included in this "plus" element in management is the characteristic that gives the executive both the desire to forge ahead when the odds are against him and the resources to make the right decisions and then see them through. It is this extra philosophical dimension that makes this book unique. In this book I have attempted to portray this "plus" factor along with a series of basic management elements which I feel are essential for overall success in management.

This volume could have been titled, "Eighteen Plus Three": eighteen basic management elements, plus three in this elusive realm of intuition and the supernatural. The eighteen basic elements are divided into six parts or "qualities" which I have called:

1. *Function Related Qualities* — *The job must be accomplished . . .*

2. *People Related Qualities* — *. . . through people . . .*

3. *Principle Related Qualities* — *. . . in a framework of responsibility . . .*

4. *Personality Related Qualities* — *. . . with the manager exhibiting outward . . .*

5. *Self Related Qualities* — *. . . and inward control . . .*

6. *Balance Related Qualities* — *. . . that avoids extremes . . .*

Most of these are generally accepted by progressive modern management as being essential elements for success in leadership. A weakness in any one of the qualities might not hinder success but would certainly weaken the overall leadership ability of that individual. For example:

★ A promoter might be weak in Function Related Qualities and strong in most others.

★ A scientist might be weak in People Related Qualities and strong in most others.

★ A politician might be weak in Principle Related Qualities and strong in most others.

★ A philosopher might be weak in Personality Related Qualities and strong in most others.

But to be a true leader in almost any field of endeavor a person must have strengths in all six areas. To those not naturally endowed or trained to adequate strength in these qualities, there is, however, a seventh strength, which I have called:

7. *Special "Plus"*   *. . . and has that supreme pur-*
   Qualities   *pose, direction and motivation.*

This quality can act as a catalyst or even as a compensator for weakness, creating a total leadership quality that could not have existed otherwise.

Of course, there is that rare individual who has dedicated himself to training, to principles and to mankind. He has developed all seven of the quality areas to a high degree. From the history of our nation I would not attempt to place more than a dozen men in this category. But it is, nevertheless, an attainable goal.

The potential of such outstanding leadership is still available to anyone, regardless of race, color or environment, if the desire and motivation are present and the special qualities set forth in this book are accepted as the framework for development. Within this framework, such leadership is within the grasp of all.

I do not claim to have mastered all the elements of success presented herein, but I recognize their value and their necessity and continue to press for their development in my own career. They are presented here so that you, too, can join with me in this development.

I have long been interested in management and people, and have studied at great length in this area. Repeatedly, I have seen this undefinable "plus" force at work. If you, like many others, are puzzled and are wondering what is that extra "something," that "plus" that makes men succeed, and along with it gives them peace, happiness and a real purpose in life, then I would urge you to read this book carefully and, by all means, put it into practice in your life.

INTRODUCTION

Management is a much used (and often abused) term. The image of the word conveys such concepts as financial "power," upper class, capitalism, stock market, etc. In reality, management is none of these things. It is simply the science (or "art" as some would justifiably say) of getting things done through people.

No manager ever achieves greatness by having produced a product or a service with his own two hands. He depends on others, usually hundreds or thousands of others, and sometimes even hundreds of thousands. His basic skill lies in inspiring and directing people to do the things he has envisioned can be done with the facilities and resources available to him. For this reason, management really has no exclusive relationship to business or industry. True, it generally focuses there, but this is only because it is business and industry where larger groups of people are often pulled together for a common goal of producing a product or service. As a result, the leadership qualities necessary to accomplish this goal are in greater demand in this field.

But management is a skill needed and used in all professions where people are gathered together for a common purpose. A hospital requires management of its staff, its nurses and even management of its doctors (a sometimes difficult task). A large church, entailing a staff of several people, requires management. The various levels and echelons of government also demand good management.

Therefore, management is not necessarily just a business profession, it is a profession that is applicable wherever there are things to do and people to do them. And with the world's population continuing to increase, the demand for good management will most certainly continue.

What is good management and how can it be acquired? There are many colleges and graduate schools which offer scores of lengthy and complex courses dealing with the details and concepts of what management is and how to apply it. This book does not attempt to cover the entire scope or the many ramifications of management, particularly the technical procedures and the analytical processes that are so much in use today. Instead, this book deals primarily with some basic concepts or the framework upon which a management philosophy must be built.

To accomplish this, it is necessary to begin with you as an individual, assuming that you desire to build into yourself good management procedures. It is necessary for you to examine your preparedness and knowledge of what management is and the rigors it requires (Part One), your attitudes toward people (Part Two), your willingness to subject yourself to the responsibilities of management (Part Three), your emotional drive and ability to control your emotions (Part Four), your basic attitudes toward yourself (Part Five), your sense of balance and judgment for specific situations (Part Six), and that special *plus* quality for which this entire book has been written. This is not only the most important dimension but with it you can easily create additional strengths in the other six areas.

It is my firm conviction that all of these principles put to constructive use will give you a leadership quality which is unmatched. Whether you are the president of a large corporation, a college administrator, the owner of a small business, or the foreman in a labor gang, the principles are all the same and are all equally applicable.

The actual grouping of these various elements or characteristics is not as precise as the group titles might indicate. The difference between some groups is small and between some there is considerable overlap. Thus the groupings I have utilized and even the specific characteristics set forth are not intended to be definitive in nature or even complete and all encompassing. They are designed to be more general and typical in terms of your relationship to your job, to people, to principles, and to yourself. The result is an informal and natural grouping and is an identification based on my experiences in more than twenty years of management in industry, business, education, churches, civic and professional organizations.

The number "three" is often referred to as the number of completion, and the number "seven" as the number of perfection. So the goal of this book is that each segment with its three qualities will be complete, and that the seventh segment, the "plus" segment, will add that dimension to management desirable for everyone who must, in everyday working situations, "get things done through people."

Part One

FUNCTION RELATED QUALITIES

This first group of characteristics is related to the job itself or the basic functions to be performed in the job (and your relationship to these functions). They appear first in the book since in almost any order of importance the highest priority goes to "getting the job done." This does not mean that the job should get done regardless of *how* it is done or regardless of what means are used in getting it done. It does mean that if the job does not get done then the other things become irrelevant because you have failed in your basic task (and either the job no longer exists or you have been removed from it).

So in all the careful analysis that you give to the various concepts and characteristics that follow in this book, it is absolutely essential to remember that the job must still get done. Neither is this concept incompatible with what is presented throughout the book. At points it may seem so, but in all cases the principles outlined can be applied and relied upon to assist in getting things done. To do this, it is necessary to view the characteristic being discussed, not as a rule, but as a guide. It must be adapted and adjusted with sincerity so that the job at hand may be accomplished.

This tendency will be dealt with at some length in later parts of the book.

Too many people become extremists in their job. Such people are either tough and ruthless taskmasters or they assume a sweet and docile "Mr. Milquetoast" personality. In reality, it is not necessary to go to either extreme, nor is it good to ride in the middle and be what some might call a continuous compromiser. Both types of leadership (firm and loose) are necessary and good at times and it is of vital importance to know *when* each is necessary.

The real emphasis, therefore, should not be placed on just getting the job done, but more on doing so with maximum utilization of the qualities and characteristics outlined herein.

The functions to be considered in any job will vary radically depending on the job itself. Some jobs will require an individual with a great deal of formal training such as a college or graduate degree. The dean of an engineering school, for example, must be highly educated himself to deal adequately with the people and problems of his job. The football or basketball coach might require a great deal of practical experience or personal skill. A top executive in a major business firm might require a long period of development, education, training and experience.

Therefore, the functions required by your particular profession or occupation will actually determine the specifics of that preparation or training. This you probably already know. In this book, then, we will deal mainly with the more general approach necessary in these functional aspects of getting the job done.

The possession of a basic technical knowledge
of your specialty field and the "rules"
of the game so that errors of ignorance
are not compounded upon the allowable and
sometimes unavoidable errors in judgment.

I.

CAPABILITY

In any managing situation you must first have the basic
competence the job itself demands and be able to attain
the level of performance the job requires. This I choose
to call capability. In its largest sense, capability could actually cover the entire range of abilities set forth in this
book. In the narrowest sense, capability deals with the
technical competence of the individual along with his desire
and ability to gain that competence in the minimum period
of time (if he does not have it when going into a job).
A manager must be equipped with many talents, or at least
he must seem to have many talents. In a business situation,
he must, of course, have a strong financial background.
In fact, in almost any management situation, (whether it
be a church, school, hospital, institution or industry), a
basic and thorough knowledge of accounting and basic
financial principles is a must. While controllers, treasurers
and accountants can be engaged to do most of the detail
work of financial accounting, unless the manager has sufficient knowledge to guide the financial affairs in relationship
to all of his other decisions, he is operating under a severe
handicap.

This does not mean that every manager must be a trained
accountant or that unless you are a trained accountant you

can never reach that top position. If you are observant
about management positions, however, and the men who
fill them, I am sure you have noticed an unusually large
number of "financial" or financially oriented people in the
top spots. This is not by accident, nor is it any kind of
manipulation. It is simply that if you have a solid grasp of
its financial affairs, you are more able to run an organization
and make its major decisions. If you are not a trained accountant or if you have not specialized in this field in some
way, then your first decision is to enroll in a course in basic
finance and accounting at a local college or in one of the
many excellent correspondence schools. This is an absolute
must if you really want to be a manager. There is just no
way you can manage effectively, regardless of the type of
organization, without some basic knowledge in this field.
Much can be absorbed by careful and patient listening to
those responsible for the finances of your organization and
you should observe them. But this area is of sufficient importance to require some formal training. Lest you think
I am pushing my own specialty here, let me add that my
basic education and training has not been in finance. I have
had to gain this knowledge the hard way and have always
been desirous of more capability in this area.

Other areas of capability as far as technical competence
is concerned may depend largely on the type of organization. In an engineering consulting firm, the manager must
have some strong engineering capabilities. Without these
he would be unable to evaluate the performance of his
people or the relationships with his customers. The same
would be true of a manufacturing manager. He needs
basic knowledge of manufacturing processes. Or a hospital
administrator needs a basic knowledge of medical procedures, and a retail business manager must have a basic
knowledge of retailing. This basic information is usually
gained through years of exposure in an organization as a
person works his way up through the ranks. Normally this
is no problem, because frequently this is the route the
manager follows in reaching his job. Occasionally, however,

a person for one reason or another is thrust into a job in which he lacks this basic orientation or exposure. In such an instance, your procedure becomes critical.

The first rule in such a situation is to listen intently. This cannot be overemphasized. The newly appointed manager who insists on continuously talking and dominating his situation for fear someone will find out he does not know the technical side of his job is in trouble from the start. His men will more quickly detect his lack of knowledge if he talks than they will if he listens. And then they will lose respect for him also because he is trying to bluff rather than to admit he doesn't have the knowledge. An honest approach is necessary. It was Abraham Lincoln who wisely said, "You may fool all the people some of the time; you can even fool some of the people all of the time; but you can't fool all of the people all of the time." Attempting to "fake" what you do not know is a dangerous practice in which many are tempted to engage. Don't! It will almost always catch up with you.

I am not saying you must announce to everyone your ignorance of certain things, for this would be equally bad. But it does mean that you listen as intently as you are able and comment as little as possible until you know what you are saying. This is why it is always a good policy in a strange situation to maintain status quo for a sufficient length of time to allow for absorption of this basic knowledge.

Sometimes a particular situation demands that you take a strong positive position at the beginning and show a strong hand at the outset (there are such instances, but fewer than you might think). If you are otherwise qualified to "manage," then it is all the more imperative that you have the basic knowledge of the operations prior to assuming such responsibilities. Here again, some basic courses at a local college or in a correspondence course can help you if you have the time and advance notice to do so.

I will never forget my own first "management" experience. The term "cultural shock" is used a great deal today.

Well, what I ran into was "management shock." I had been reared next door to my father's factory, had played around machinery and knew the basic controls on the lathe from the age of seven or eight years, and had been foreman over a small machine shop group at eighteen. Still I had never really "managed."

At twenty-four I had been out of the service just a couple of years, doing tool engineering work without much responsibility. I was just on the verge of going back to school to continue my academic work. Dad called me in one day and said, "Rich, we've got some problems over in the Vicksburg plant and we just can't seem to get it going like it should. You seem to be pretty well organized and analytical and, besides that, it's time you got your feet wet. I want you to go over to Vicksburg and take over the plant as General Manager."

That scuttled my college plans. So with my wife (we had been married only two years) and one-year-old son, and with much fear and trembling, I moved to Vicksburg. In retrospect I guess the fear and trembling of the supervisors in that plant was greater than mine at the prospect of the boss's twenty-four-year-old son becoming manager.

However, I had already learned I didn't know much, so I did two things: I studied hard and listened hard. Immediately I enrolled in a correspondence course in accounting and finance (I knew absolutely nothing about either field). When decisions needed to be made, I would not only ask the department head for his recommendations but I would ask him to explain why he felt as he did in great detail. That way I could learn how his area functioned.

Not every manager has the "opportunity" for this kind of shock learning but it demonstrates the importance of being ready.

The primary thing to be kept in mind here is that there are many things in management which cannot be learned except by experience and making mistakes. In these areas of technical capability, however, you must learn as much as possible by some other process. If you attempt to gain all your technical competence through this same experience and mistake-making progress (as you learn the other "people handling" chores of a manager), then you will probably make so many mistakes you will never make it very far up the ladder. Only a certain number of mistakes will be permitted by your boss. He will understand some of your judgment errors in handling people, but he will probably be very intolerant in the technical competence area. Here, with a little effort, you could have avoided mistakes.

Fortunately for me, the people with whom I worked, both immediately above and below me, were very understanding (the boss's son, you know). With this attitude on their part I learned quickly and came out in fine shape. You might not be as fortunate as I, however.

It is surprising to me how many people want to be managers or want to be given positions of leadership, yet how few are willing to subject themselves to the stringent training so obviously required to prepare them for such positions. Management is not an easy job. It takes hard work to prepare for it, and it's hard work after you get there.

Someone has said that as a laborer he worked eight hours a day, was paid overtime, and had no worries; now as the boss he works sixteen hours a day, without overtime pay, and has all the worries. So, if you're not willing to subject yourself to the hard work of preparation or the prospect of sixteen hours per day with ulcer potentials, then management is not for you. A manager *must* be capable and dedicated to getting the job done.

The ability to create, when the situation
warrants, a tough and exacting requirement
of people and functions.

2

TOUGH - ABILITY

Sometimes, to get the job done, it is necessary for us to
become tough and demanding. This can be especially true
in jobs where time pressures are critical or where people
have for some reason become lax or indifferent. This fact
may seem a bit incongruous in the light of the rest of the
book, but it is, nevertheless, important for you as a successful manager to remember it. Its application requires
a great deal of judgment and its application will also vary
considerably with different types of organizations and situations. But even in the most benevolent type of organization, such as a church or church-related situation, there
are conditions which will eventually require you to be tough
and exacting in your requirements of people and functions.

In business and industry the obvious motive and necessity for this "toughness" is the fact that unless the business
earns a profit it will cease to exist within a short period
of time. And to be consistently profitable in an organization
made up of different types of people with different motivations, it will become necessary for you to be tough and
demanding at various times — or possibly even continuously
tough and demanding. This is not necessarily inconsistent
with the tone of the remainder of this book. But if a situation requires such a stance, it will undoubtedly make the
rest of this book more difficult to apply. It will require

some real concentration on your part, and emphasis on all the characteristics set forth herein.

Even in philanthropic institutions or church organizations, an administrator must be capable of being tough on occasion. Surely, this action is not necessary as often as it is in a profit-making business. But time pressures are frequently present even in such "non-profit" organizations. Without definite requirements, people will take advantage of the leader at some point and make his functions less effective than desirable. In many organizations, the "people relations" will, of course, predominate and most problems or difficulties will be solved by discussion, consultation and compromises. But even then, a good administrator must know when to draw a halt to the discussion-negotiation procedure and lay down the requirements and decisions best for the organization.

Once in a discussion with a college administrator, I was referring to this phenomenon whereby even in church-related institutions it is sometimes necessary to "get tough." The administrator indicated he had always been able to solve his problems with people by the discussion method. Because of his personal expertise in "people handling" during a number of years in college administration, he had never had to fire a man. To me, rather than an indication of strength, this was an indication of weakness. It indicated to me that he would go to great lengths to avoid breaking his record of never firing a man. In so doing he could very possibly bring great harm to his organization and to other people. This does not mean that firing a man is an enjoyable exercise. Certainly it is not! Nor does it mean it is always necessary to fire people to show that you are doing a good job. That also would be an immature position to hold. What it does mean is that you must be willing to do so if it is necessary for the good of the organization and the other people in it. Your attitude should be such that you do not have any "hang-ups" in this area. Incidentally, several years later this same administrator, (when his lack of toughness began to get him in trouble) realized

exactly what I am saying here and has as a result become
a much better administrator.

Many people do not understand that, in a profit-making
organization or business, the profits are the reason the business exists. A proprietor invests his funds in a business for
only one purpose — to get a return on his investment, a
profit. And this profit must be greater generally than that
available to him from other more secure or low-risk in-
vestments such as savings accounts, bonds, etc. You as a
manager are, therefore, responsible and accountable to produce a return on this investment even if it means you must
be tough and exacting and sometimes misunderstood by
those with whom you work. What happens if you balk at
this? What happens if you allow your super-consideration
for people always to rule? What happens if you refuse
to make changes or discharge an old-time employee when
he is not producing? One of two alternatives becomes prob-
able. Your superiors, whether it be the boss or the board
of directors of the company, will find it necessary to discharge you when you fail to make a profit (and put someone else in your place who will show a profit). Or the
company will eventually go bankrupt and cease to exist.
In this case, many others besides the one in question will
also lose their jobs. So your being a "good guy" in such a
case does not change anything.

Of course, there are many situations where required action of this type is not so simple nor quite as easily identified with the organization's survival. In these cases, you
must use judgment and establish a style of management
by which each member of the management team includes
this "tough-ability" characteristic, along with the others,
for a leadership of maximum effectiveness.

Neither should you allow yourself to get into a position
of being forced to fire a man for non-production without
first helping him to overcome his difficulty and giving him
an opportunity to improve.

My father, R. G. LeTourneau, was known throughout his
lifetime for his Christian witness as well as for his genius

and progress in building a great manufacturing concern. He had many demands made upon him for philantrophic causes which he had to refuse. Also, he was often criticized by people who felt that as a Christian and a philanthropist, he should not be as hard on his employees as he often was. His answer to this was, "If I gave to everything people felt I should give to, or if. I was as considerate of people as some thought I should be, my business would go broke and there wouldn't be any profits to do the things I am now doing. And there wouldn't be any jobs either, for me to give people, so that I could be considerate!"

So, while being considerate is important, as you will see by the great emphasis on this factor in later chapters. This characteristic must fall into a proper relationship with the running of the buisness itself (or run the risk of causing much greater inequities than the execution of a tough but mature management decision). Therefore, it is of utmost importance that a successful manager learn how to be tough and exacting of people and functions when the situation warrants.

A recognition that the way others do it,
or the way you did it successfully once before,
is not always the best way to do it now.

3.

FLEXIBILITY

We come now to the third in the "job related" characteristics which are important to you as a manager. This one
deals with your general approach to the details, procedures,
methods and policies which are a daily part of your job.
A big danger in writing a management book (or any "how-
to-do-it" book for that matter) is that we are apt to establish a set of rules by which to operate without using judgment or flexibility in the particular situation where we
are applying them. This cannot be done. Any situation
that deals with decisions based on judgment or on the
reactions of people cannot be defined sufficiently that a
given set of rules will always work. And this book is certainly no exception. What is set forth in this book is, at
best, a guide to give you a better understanding of the
processes involved in management. Any decision in any
situation must then be modified by the particular circumstances surrounding that situation and the personalities of
the people involved. This means that "flexibility" takes
on an important role in management. Adjustments must
be made continually to maintain good leadership.

Books, or even the advice of people, can only help in
giving a general framework for good management. Or
they can provide important limits which should be exceeded
only for good reason. In doing so, books create in you an

"attitude" of managing that will allow you the flexibility with which you must operate. At the same time abiding by general guidelines prevents you from making some of the more obvious mistakes that have plagued others.

This attitude of "flexibility" is important even beyond its reference to the guides and rules you must use. It also extends to those concepts and experiences developed within your own career. Many times a concept or procedure will work perfectly one time and fail miserably the next. Why is this? Frequently it is because different people are involved, and they react differently. Also, the lapse of time between situations makes a difference. Circumstances may have changed to the degree that what worked once will not work again. I have found this true even in the designing of simple forms, the format of a report, a financial statement, the rules of thumb used for inventory control or a myriad of other similar things. Each time a matter is approached it must be approached with an open mind. Not that it *must* be changed each time, but a good manager will not get in the rut of saying, "That's the way we've always done it," and use that as a reason for not analyzing his situation more carefully.

For instance, there are certain basic concepts of organization which seem to work best and which I have generally tried to follow (such as never having a person reporting to more than one man). On several occasions, however, due to the nature of the job to be done and the personalities of the people involved, I have quite successfully violated that rule. To have held to the rule would have meant a less than effective organization in *that particular instance*. At some other time, or with some other people or with some other functions involved, such a move may have resulted in chaos. To do this too frequently in an organization might create problems as well.

Here again, judgment becomes highly important and a balance must be obtained. This will be pointed out in a later chapter in a discussion of flexibility and too much status quo or getting into a rut. Each situation must be analyzed in its own light with mature judgment and a willingness to change if necessary. Yet you must maintain a stability that speaks of sound leadership.

Closely coupled with this matter of flexibility is the undeniable fact that our society is in the midst of a period of rapid and even radical change. Much has been written regarding both the necessity of change and the recognition of it in the various facets of our life and work. The rub comes when change is pitted against human nature's resistance to it. To resist change (as many do) in our modern business society, however, is to die a slow death. On the other hand, changing too rapidly and getting ahead of the mainstream of society can cause equally catastrophic problems. Here's where the flexibility and judgment come in. It becomes an attitude, not a process. There must be a *willingness* to change without the *compulsion* to change. Change is good and necessary to get one out of a rut, or to alter an ineffective pattern of operation. It is bad, however, if carried to the extreme. Here it may create such confusion that good business practices cannot be followed.

As I was writing this chapter, a horrible example of too much change or flexibility crossed my desk. In the manufacture of heavy construction equipment, good dealers who sell our equipment are a vital part of the business. Yet just this month we lost an excellent dealer. He quit us. Why? Because we kept changing. We changed models of machines. We changed our minds on the terms of sale. We changed our sales and service personnel several times. Finally, he threw up his hands in disgust. He was through.

Now, we had good reasons for every change we made. And we ended up having to make some more changes to correct the problems created by the previous changes. But while we understood what we were doing each time (at least I think we did) the dealer certainly didn't understand it and we lost him.

Moderation and caution are essential in change. One should maintain an attitude of flexibility without the recklessness and compulsion that sometimes creeps in.

Part Two

PEOPLE RELATED QUALITIES

Next in importance to the functional aspects of your job and actually "getting it done" is the people through whom you must work to accomplish your task. Without the co-operation of people, the accomplishment of a job becomes difficult or almost impossible. Thus, while "getting the job done" is the first priority, the second priority, "through people," is of sufficient magnitude that it must be treated as nearly equal in importance.

"People" are not strange creatures through whom you are forced to operate. They are not even the impersonal "employees" or "subordinates" who always do the wrong thing, or at least something different than was expected. People are really no different than you are yourself. They are human beings, subject to the same emotions, misunderstandings, misapprehensions, confusion, fatigue, and motivation (or lack thereof) that you are. In other words, they are persons just like you and me and they like to be treated the same way we like to be treated. They like to have clear instructions (or clearly understood latitude of actions when instructions are not clear) just as we prefer to have. They want to follow a well organized leader who knows what he is doing, just as you do not want to work under a disorganized, helter-skelter boss. They want their manager to understand their particular problems and needs the same as you want your boss to understand your personal needs which should be taken into consideration when he makes demands of you.

That's what the game of managing people is all about. Whether it is the big boss himself, a middle line manager or the man carrying out the day-to-day functions of a job, all are "people" with minds, hearts, emotions, and bodies. They require communication, organization and understanding. That's what this segment is all about — "people."

The ability to communicate with others,
in all situations, both verbally and in writing,
so that clear intent is transmitted in both directions
without misinterpretation by either party.

4

COMMUNICATE - ABILITY

Probably the greatest cause of breakdowns in the relationships of people in a company, in a nation, or between nations is a lack of communication (or poor communication).

Communication is a subject on which many volumes have been written. I have written much on it myself. But in this context, it will be treated only briefly and to the point. Without communication it would be almost impossible for any job requiring more than one person to get done. And communicating is not the simple process it appears to be at first glance. Let's break down the process that takes place in all comunication whether it be oral or written.

To begin with you have an idea, a concept or a thought in your mind. To communicate this to another person, it is first necessary for you to convert this into specific words. This conversion or translation process is based on the use of words and the meaning that you place on them. This comes from your own culture, background and experience. The person to whom the communication is directed then hears or reads these words and translates them back into ideas, concepts or thoughts in his mind. But the problem is that he does not always attach the same meanings to your words as you do (because of his different culture, background and experience). In the process of going through two translations where the basis of translation is not the same, the original ideas, concepts or thoughts frequently are confused and do not come through clearly. For example, Webster's unabridged dictionary gives seventy-three different meanings of the word "round," and there are hundreds of words in common English usage that are nearly as complex.

With this complication in mind, let's go a step further and discuss briefly the difference between written and oral communication. In oral communication there is the obvious advantage that the words carry with them tones or inflections which can assist greatly in conveying the intended meaning. In addition, if the oral communication is face to face (rather than by phone), expressions and gestures can be helpful in conveying the true meaning intended. However, there are some disadvantages in oral communication. These can be overcome if the communication is written. In oral communication you quickly forget the words and remember only the thought which those words conveyed to you. As you reflect on what was said you may read a different interpretation into the message. Since the specific words have been forgotten, you may begin to read into it something entirely different from what was intended. Or you may forget what was perceived originally from tone, expression or gestures.

Written words, too, can create problems but in a different way. The reader can re-read a written message several times over a period of time and may pick at words to the point that even though he correctly read the intended meaning the first time, his re-reading may convince him of another and unintended meaning.

What all this means is that extreme care must be taken to insure that intended meanings are conveyed. One of the best methods of insuring this (although still not infallible) is through feedback or two-way communication. Through exchanges of words and repetition of thoughts back to the originator, the clarity of a message may often be assured.

This is why, when giving important instructions to someone, it is always best to ask him to repeat the instructions back to you rather than just accepting his "yeah," or nod of the head. Many people *think* they understand, but they have missed the point or key instructions completely.

The other day I called one of my associates in a different city and related an important matter to him. He was to discuss this with one of his men and call me back with a decision. I did not take the time to ascertain that he had understood the intent of the matter, but just assumed he was listening carefully. Later he became involved in other details and asked his man to call me back with the answer. I was appalled. Either my associate was not listening to me or he sure muffed it when he conveyed the message to his man. By now, the matter was chaotic. As a result I had to make another call to straighten out a situation that was rapidly becoming difficult.

But then there is more to communication and communicate-ability than the mechanics of words and meanings between two people. The development and operation of communication networks within any organization becomes an essential part of the success of that organization. There are both formal and informal communications and both are essential in a healthy organization. Communication also flows in different directions. It can flow downward from the boss to the employees. This is the only kind that exists in some organizations. Also, it can (and should) flow upward from the employees to the boss or top management. Then, too, there is the cross-flow of communication between the same levels of the organization. All of these are vital and necessary in a well-run system.

For an employee to do his best and be effective in an organization, he must first identify himself with it. He must feel he is a desirable and needed part of it, that he belongs. To develop this feeling, there must be open two-way communication available to him, as to the affairs and business of the organization. In a large company this may take several forms, such as mailings to the employee's home with company reports, newsletters, etc. Bulletin boards and communication through the various levels of supervision are also effective. The method is not necessarily critical. The main thing is to communicate honestly and make all employees feel they are a part of the organization.

Channels upward must be kept open also. This does not mean you must have an "open door policy" so that every Tom, Dick and Harry who has a gripe can go around those in authority over him to get to you. But it does mean that at all levels of supervision, there must be an attitude of receptiveness to the legitimate problems and gripes of employees so that the employees do not feel the necessity of circumventing those in authority.

Informal communication is also a necessary part of the communication system. Many managers try to wipe out the informal system because they feel it carries too many rumors and misinformation. This is wrong! First of all, it cannot be eliminated. The "grapevine" will continue to operate regardless of pressures to the contrary! In fact, the more pressure to eliminate it, the better it will thrive. What's more, if there are enough different rumors, some are certain to be true and you will always have some people who can say, "I told you so! I knew it all along!" They didn't really know, but with a given number of alternatives and a large number of people guessing, someone will be right. And people guess more intelligently than you may think, too.

Secondly, the best and only right way to get rid of the rumors and misinformation is to disseminate correct information. People must have information. If you do not furnish it, someone will make conjectures and the discussions that follow the conjectures will lend credence to them. In no time at all, such misinformation can become the "official word" from management. A good manager does not consider informal communication as an evil to be tolerated. Rather, he considers it one of the most valuable tools of his people relationships and utilizes it to its fullest by seeing to it that this pipeline contains plenty of interesting, stimulating and honest material.

Cross communication within management is another vital element of a successful organization. In a large organization, this is particularly necessary, because of the large and constant volume of decisions which must be made daily to carry on the business. Many of these decisions are made only after cross-level communication between line and staff personnel or between others on similar levels. Included in this area of communication are meetings, brainstorming sessions, luncheon discussions, written memos, phone calls, etc. Also generally falling within this type of cross-level communication, are structured committee or group meetings. At this point, discussion of the usefulness and dangers of committees in this context would be very helpful to you as a manager.

There are several types of committees generally used in organizational structures. This includes a board of control which is actually a committee operating at the head of an organization. Before identifying the various types of committees and their specific duties, let me identify the particular functions in which committees excel and those in which they may have difficulty. Because a committee is a group of individuals (usually from three to thirty, but it can be much larger), it takes on different characteristics from those of an individual and must be evaluated differently.

In many ways a committee can be invaluable because it makes available a wider scope of knowledge and avoids the biases that might be present in an individual. Contrari-wise, because of the variety of opinions and the difficulty both in making decisions and in being held responsible for them, a committee can be slower acting and less effective in certain instances and will only rarely give real leadership to an organization.

Generally speaking and in an all-inclusive sense, committees are excellent in the following functions:

* Communicating   * Recommending
* Discussing   * Evaluating
* Advising   * Exercising judgment

On the other hand, committees are normally poor when they are required to:

★ Give leadership   ★ Exercise authority
★ Assume responsibility   ★ Make prompt decisions
★ Take action

There are exceptions to these rules, of course, but if we recognize the type of functions committees generally do well or poorly, then we can better deal with them in specific applications and utilize them wisely within an organization.

In a dynamic or autocratic organization, any committees permitted would necessarily stay strictly within the above functional limits. In a democratic or socially oriented organization, there would be a much broader interpretation of committee limitations.

In a more tightly structured organization the basic problem with committees is that for a decision-making entity (individual or committee) to be given authority to take action and make decisions, it must also be able to be held "responsible" for the results of that decision or action. Whereas individuals can receive positive or negative rewards as a result of their actions and decisions, a committee cannot. Thus no discipline can be applied to a committee functioning within the hierarchy of an organization. When this type of control of the committee is not necessary, then the limitations of committees begins to diminish.

The type of committee and its specific duties also become important in evaluating its ability to function effectively. While it is difficult to classify committees accurately, I will attempt to do so in a broad sense to help clarify my comments on them. Broadly, these committees are:

Board of Control. This is a very important, perhaps the most important type of committee. Any organization responsible to public interest (investment money from the public or a democratic social or governmental organization) generally has as its supreme head a committee which can exercise broad judgment and knowledge in controlling the organization to the best interest of its own public. Normally these individuals are elected by the public to whom they are responsible. Thus, to a degree, they are subject to the "responsibility" concepts above and can, in effect, be rewarded positively (re-elected) or negatively (not re-elected). They are therefore able to function properly, even in most functions where committees are normally weak.

Even this type of committee cannot give leadership, however. Leadership must come from a single individual at the head of the organization or the committee.

Service Committee. Many organizations form committees for the specific purpose of accomplishing certain tasks with each member of the committee normally acting as an individual in performing a portion of those tasks but coordinating them with the others through the committee. In this sense the committee functions primarily as a coordinating device. An example of this might be a church dinner food committee, with each member responsible for certain contacts or certain foods for the dinner.

Narrow Task Committee. Certain narrowly defined tasks in an organization may require the collective judgment of several individuals. If these tasks are specific then a committee can still function well even in the action and decision area. An example of this type could be a finance committee which oversees certain types of expenditures within the limits of authority granted to it by its higher authority. In such areas it can exercise judgment and make decisions within specifically defined limits.

Advisory Committee. This is the type of committee which does very well in that it carries no responsibility, is required to take no action, yet it can discuss, communicate and make recommendations to the responsible individual in the organization. Many times these committees make recommendations that are tantamount to decisions since their recommendations may be almost always accepted.

Yet the actual decision, authority and responsibility rests with an individual. A wise administrator will make frequent use of this type of committee to maximize both communication with his cohorts and the utilization of their knowledge and judgment.

Internal Control Committee.   A committee which has broad decision-making authority and is within the organizational structure (not at the head of it) can be a very dangerous committee and only in rare cases should a committee of this type be allowed to operate in a dynamic organization. Because such committees bring a potential direct conflict with the structured hierarchy of the organization, where they are used extensively, they tend to clog the machinery and increase the bickering and "politicking" in an organization.

Unfortunately most religious and educational organizations are beseiged with a host of this type of committee. This is probably the largest single cause for the lack of more dynamic organizations in these areas.

For example, in education a faculty committee that decided whether a course in history should include a greater emphasis on one era or another would be a "narrow task" committee and as long as they stayed within the limitations imposed by the philosophy of the school, they could function well. But if this committee had the authority to add courses or curricula which could affect broad areas of finance, planning and efficiency, it would be a dangerous "internal control" committee. If, on the other hand, its function was to evaluate the need for course and curricula additions and then make recommendations to the proper individual in the organizational hierarchy, it becomes an "advisory" committee and can be highly effective.

The important thing in using committees is to make certain you know which type of committee you have formed and then make certain all committee members know the uses and limitations of the committee which has been established. Committees, therefore, function in many ways in many different situations and one of their most effective uses is that of communication.

To summarize, communication in management is a translation process. It is a two-way exchange of concepts and ideas with expressions and hidden meanings. Communication can be oral or written with advantages and disadvantakes in both methods. In an organization it is both formal and informal. It can be between two or more individuals, or between groups and committees. In committees, make sure that the communication you hope to accomplish does not backfire through an inappropriate application of the "committee" concept. Communication travels up, down and crosswise in the organization and takes many forms which are necessary and valuable, but it must be used properly.

Communicate-ability is thus the ability to communicate clearly to others with whom you work by the various means and methods available.

The ability to coordinate people and
arrange logically for review, decision and follow-up,
all of the myriads of functions and details
that confront any worthwhile enterprise.

5.

ORGANIZE-ABILITY

Probably one of the characteristics that helps most in developing the good communication we have been talking about is the ability to organize systematically what is to be communicated and then develop a sound logical plan for doing so. To do this requires a high degree of organization both of functions and people.

Being "organized" or "disorganized" seems to be an inborn trait. Some of us seem to have an uncanny ability or desire to see things in order and all details cared for meticulously. Others of us, regardless of how hard we try, just cannot seem to keep things in logical order. Undoubtedly, some of this is related to individual personality, yet a great deal is related to early training and the habits of parents in the home life. This desire, or lack of desire, to have things neat and in order, continues on into our ability to organize many functions or care for many details. Whether ability to organize is naturally present or not, does not negate the fact that it is still a necessary element in managing. If we don't naturally have organize-ability then its importance to us actually increases. For then it becomes necessary for us to make a definite effort to correct the deficiency and force ourselves to give more attention to this area.

I am not talking particularly about a clear and orderly

desk, although this is generally an indicator. You *can* have a messy *appearing* desk and yet be very systematically and logically organized as far as you are concerned. But if vital information gets misplaced frequently, if you continually forget to do something important or if you lose reminder notes of critical appointments or "things to do," then you have problems.

This does not necessarily mean that a disorganized person cannot be a good manager. As with many of the other characteristics set forth in this book, it is quite possible to be a good manager even though you are weak in this one area. However, it is definitely more difficult to be a good manager when this handicap of poor organization must be overcome.

Another point: organization as a term does not mean just keeping things in systematic order. It means as well the ability to do several things at once and keep them all in your mind (or your notebook) and keep the proper priorities assigned to each. It also means getting people to work together without conflict and making sure that there are no gaps or overlaps in the assignment of functions to them.

A person who is well organized, and who is able to organize people and functions, should excel in the following areas:

a) LOGIC. You should be capable of thinking logically, visualizing in your mind the next step and the various alternatives to a particular situation, analyzing them without emotion and weighing the pro's and con's without rationalizing.

b) DETAILS. You should make sure that nothing is overlooked that is important to the carrying out of your job. If you cannot trust your memory then you should devise a system of notes or memory "joggers" so that none will be omitted.

c) DEFINITION. You should make certain that your instructions are clear and precise and that they

are understood properly. (Communication!)
Vague, poorly transmitted or misunderstood directions are the cause of much confusion and dis-
organization.

d) DECISIVENESS. Probably nothing will cause as
much difficulty in an organization as a manager
who cannot, or will not, make decisions when they
are needed. Of course, decisions should not be
made until all the facts of a situation are gathered.
But after all the information relative to a decision
has been gathered, an indecisive manner on your
part can be disastrous.

e) ORDERLINESS. You should do first things first and
not let your priorities of importance get out of
line. Usually you should have a check list for
every major project you tackle. This may be in
a notebook or could even be in your mind, but
regardless of the media you use, you should methodically make sure all items are covered.

A word about organization "charts" is important here.
Some managers feel that without well defined and tightly
structured charts showing every person's relationship to
every other person in the organization, a business just
cannot operate effectively. In some cases this is true. Other
managers insist on the flexibility and informality that can
be attained by not putting any such chart on paper for
anyone to see and complain about. This position is also
legitimate in some cases. Whether to use a formal chart
or not must be a judgment decision in each particular case.
What is important, however, is that you have a well defined concept of your organization in your own mind and
that each person in the organization knows specifically to
whom he is responsible. If he is responsible to more than
one person there should be a good reason for this. Normally
this kind of situation leads to problems, but in some cases
it can be tolerated. Frequently, when a person is respon-

sible in more than one direction, he is given a direct responsibility to one person and a "dotted line" responsibility to another. Generally, this would mean he would take instructions and directions from both and in case of conflict would follow the "solid line" channel. This also could mean that in personnel matters, such as hours, pay, routine responsibilities, etc., he follows the "solid line," but has a staff relationship or special assignment duty to the "dotted line."

The existence of a chart is not the critical point in an organization, however. If a chart helps to define relationships properly and is not apt to cause dissension between people, then, by all means, prepare a chart. If you can accomplish the same thing without putting it on paper, and if putting it on paper might cause some petty jealousies, then forget it, it's not that important in itself.

The format or layout of an organization chart can also be important in some instances. If people are "level" conscious, you may want to turn the chart sideways. It is amazing how much less significant "levels" are in the identical chart if it is drawn crossways rather than up and down a sheet. A circular arrangement may be used in some cases, too, with the boss in the center and those under him radiating out at different progressively larger circles around him. Then, too, if you have a particular individual whose ego you are trying to satisfy, and others in the organization do not mind a little line twisting in his favor (as long as it does not change the lines of authority in the organization), a little design work on the chart can often make him appear to be at a higher level than he really is.

How do you get organized if you are not naturally inclined that way? The only way is to make yourself do it. Get a notebook, a desk calendar, or a pocket calendar diary (there are several excellent ones on the market) and write down the things that need doing as you think of them. Do not trust your memory, regardless of how good it is. If you do not like to carry a notebook, then use 3x5 cards. Two or three of these in your shirt pocket will suffice if you conscientiously use them. Another way to overcome lack of organization is to have an assistant or secretary who is well organized and who will take care of some of these details for you. Most executives depend heavily on assistants and secretaries for this purpose. But remember, an assistant cannot read your mind (although some can come pretty close). They cannot remember for you what you do not tell them and they cannot carry out assignments of which they are unaware. So if you fall in the category of those who are "not well organized," make up your mind that you must concentrate more on this area and force yourself to do some of the things I have outlined.

Beyond being well organized in your own activities, organize-ability, as I am using the term, means being able to organize others, being able to get the right person in the right job at the right time. And because people are different and unpredictable sometimes, this is not an easy task. However, I have found that organizing people is very much akin to organizing oneself and hence, I am using this characteristic to cover both.

To get the right person in the right job at the right time, you must be able to analyze unemotionally the person involved, his strengths and weaknesses, his capabilities (both technical and in people-handling), his attitudes and his motivations. Then you must logically determine how he will fit into that particular slot, how he will react in it and how people will react to him. What I'm saying is that you, yourself, must be well organized to do this.

I can remember one of our executives, who was an extremely well qualified man in his position. He was well trained and seemed to be able to handle people well, but his organize-ability was weak. Often he would get into trouble on a major contract because he hadn't methodically checked everything out and someone had either slipped a clause in or left one out that would cause trouble. Also he wasn't as objective as he should have been on decisions, particularly those involving hiring, transferring or promoting people. He would make decisions based on whether he liked a person or whether the person had the same outside interests as he did. He also used other similar emotionally charged criteria. Needless to say, the time came when he had to be replaced. He just wasn't well enough organized in his procedures or in his thought-processes.

Organize-ability of people, functions and the daily "nitty-gritty" is thus a very essential characteristic of a good manager.

The ability to relate to people and
their needs in such a way that even a tough
and exacting manner will be recognized
as fair and empathetic.

6.

RELATE-ABILITY

While it is frequently necessary to analyze people and
attempt to predict their actions and reactions in a given
situation just as if they were a machine or computer, I
would like to raise a red caution flag at this point. The
ability to analyze and predict is not the solution to working
with people. Because each of us is a person and not a
machine, we don't react as predictably as machines do. Yet
some managers insist on treating people as if they were
mechanical robots, expecting them to perform in this precise mechanical manner. And they get upset if this is not
the case. A good manager (and a successful one) will
recognize that people are persons and must be treated as
persons — not machines.

As a manager, do you not have personal problems occasionally that affect your performance or the way you
react to people? Then, certainly you must expect those
working for you and with you to have problems also. These
can be marital problems, physical problems, child-behavior
problems, financial problems, problems with relatives or
friends, religious problems, etc. Regardless of what the
problems are, they can, at times, seriously affect the performance of an individual. As a manager, you must recognize this. It does not mean, however, that you must run a
psychological clinic for all of your employees. In fact, ex-

cept in rare cases, you should not even get involved in your employees' personal affairs. But you should recognize the *presence* of such problems and be considerate in your handling of people when such problems arise.

You cannot, however, let this fact deter you in any way from getting the job done. Nor should it deter the people who have problems from getting their jobs done. Relate-ability simply means that you need to be able to put your-self in another's place, to empathize with him sufficiently that he knows you understand and are not running rough-shod over him. You can still let him know the job must get done. In spite of his problems, he will need to under-stand that. But this communication must be done in such a way as not to be offensive to the person. Granted, it may take more of your time to communicate in this way and maybe you feel you do not have that extra time. A good manager, however, will find the time and will also realize that, in the long run, he is saving time. Satisfied and loyal employees will take less supervisory time and, with less turnover as a result, training time required for new employees is less, as well.

It doesn't take long, as you pass by an employee who has a problem, to say, "Sorry to hear about your son's ac-cident, Sam. If there is anything you need to tend to on it, feel free to take a few hours off. I would appreciate it if you would arrange to get that Acme job out before you go, though." Or if you spot an obviously troubled employee one morning you might say, "Anything wrong that I can help with, Bill?" This will be much appreciated even if you only get a "Nah" or "Uh-uh" answer.

One supervisor in our organization seemed to be a con-tinual source of trouble to everyone who had to work with him. He did an excellent job of running his department but he was a "complainer" about everything, including the way everyone else was running his department. When some-one needed him to get some work out, they would first hear all the reasons why they didn't deserve consideration and why he just couldn't get it done. If they attempted to push him or pull rank on him, it would just worsen the relationship.

But I had no trouble with him at all. Why? Because when I needed something from him I would listen patiently to all his problems and why he couldn't do it, then I would tell him, "I need this by Friday and I realize that if you can't do it you can't do it, but do the best you can, will you?" And because I had related to him and his problems by just listening, he would normally do everything possible to get the work done for me — including working unpaid overtime on it himself.

Now it's not always good business to have a man such as this in the organization. But if he's there and you can't change it, then make the best of it by relating to him. It will make your job easier.

To recap, in the interest of good employee morale and in keeping the motivation of those with whom you work high, try to "relate" to them and their problems, whether it be a work problem, a sick child, a nagging headache, an alcoholic wife, leeching in-laws, or a financial catastrophe. You, too, might find yourself in a similar situation someday and would deeply appreciate some of this same understanding from *your* boss and fellow-workers.

Part Three

PRINCIPLE RELATED QUALITIES

Now that some of the relationships to the job have been covered and the people through whom the job must be accomplished have been discussed at length, it becomes necessary to talk about some of the ways or principles to be used in "getting the job done through people."

Probably everyone would agree that the job is important and that people are important, but beyond that, managers sometimes begin to go separate ways when the discussion enters into the principles, personality and self-examination we will deal with in the next three sections. (There are some managers who will not even give credence to the importance of the previous section of this book. Even though such men may be successful in terms of financial accomplishments, they are a blight on society and the profession of management. I will not even waste space discussing their possible redemptive values to business or society).

While there may be some room for differences of opinion in the next three sections, it is my solid conviction that these characteristics are, nevertheless, essential features of the really successful manager. It is certainly possible to be successful while lacking one or more of these qualities. But in every case where there is success without these characteristics, it can be said, almost unequivocally, that the success could be greater with them. This obviously applies to all twenty-one of the qualities set forth in this book, not just those of this or any other section.

Even a manager, fully utilizing all of the "plus" qualities of Part Seven, can be a better manager by using each and every one of the other qualities set forth.

In this section, however, some basic principles of management will be covered. These are generally accepted as valid in any type of management situation. They deal with your ability to shoulder responsibility for the job you are given to do and your willingness to be held accountable for your actions and the actions of your subordinates as well. They also deal with the reliability and confidence which you exhibit in your job through the manner in which you carry it out. And they deal with the manner in which you react to the pressures or demands of your job by the stability which you exhibit in your leadership position. These then are some of the principles involved in getting the job done through people.

The ability to accept responsibility and shoulder
it squarely without passing the buck when
it falls into your realm regardless of whether
or not you could have controlled it.
"The buck stops here." — Harry Truman

7.

ACCOUNTABILITY

From the time Adam and Eve sinned in the Garden of
Eden, people have been held accountable for their actions.
In a negative sense our whole system of law and order is
based on individuals being held accountable for their actions. No substitutional accountability is allowed in our
penal system. And this concept of required accountability
plays an important role in business and industry as well.
In fact, this very complex system of rewards and punishment is what makes any organization or society function
properly.

Even socialism and communism are based on a system
of rewards and punishment. These governments may use
other media and different degrees or levels, they may use
punishment more than they do rewards, but it is the same
type of system we use in our capitalistic economy.

To make a system of rewards and punishment work
properly it is most important to be able to define specifically
who is responsible for which acts. In some organizations
this is very clear. In others it becomes a vague and complex issue. The basic problem is that no one likes to admit
he was wrong, or likes to take the blame or consequences
for his own actions, let alone take the blame for the actions
of someone else.

Conversely, of course, everyone is ready to take the credit for what went right whether he had any remote connection with it or not.

In a complex organization, however, it is often necessary for you to accept responsibility, not only for your own mistakes, but also for the mistakes of others. How can this be? It is very simple. A manager becomes responsible for the actions of every person reporting to him through all levels, as far as his own superiors are concerned. If a person under you makes a mistake, you can still hold that person accountable to you, and you can take whatever action is warranted as a result of his mistake. But as far as your boss is concerned, you alone are responsible for the mistake and he will frequently look no further down the organizational ladder than you. This may seem grossly unfair at times, but responsibility in organizations can work no other way.

Responsibility and accountability seem difficult to pin down at times because the concepts just set forth indicate that more than one person up through the organizational ladder can be responsible for the same act. This is true. But to any single person in the organization, there is only one other person responsible in a given situation. In other words, the responsibility depends on the level of observation. And from any one viewpoint, only one can be responsible. From the viewpoint of your boss, you alone are responsible for everything and every person under your direction. Then from your viewpoint, you in turn hold the persons under you responsible for their action, their area of operation, or their employees.

This fact of life must be accepted. How well it is accepted is the point of this chapter. A good manager recognizes this system and applies it to his operations both up and down the organizational ladder. If one of your employees makes a mistake that costs the company a great deal of money, you must accept that responsibility to your boss on the basis that you either (1) could have prevented it, (2) should have been running your department in such a way that it could not have happened, or (3) should not have had an employee in your group who was capable of such a mistake. At any rate, you are still accountable to your boss. The degree to which you accept this and do not try to pass the blame on to someone else will determine how good a manager you really are.

An executive with whom I am well acquainted was relieved of his position as the top man in a fair-sized manufacturing plant because of some mistakes in planning his work and the resultant sharp drop in profits that occurred. He felt this was unfair because he had inherited some of the problems from his predecessor and been directed to do some things a certain way by his superiors. When everything didn't bring forth the expected results he was blamed for the failure. My friend was probably right. It was unfair. Yet this is the risk he assumed with the job. Even though his superior may have been unjust in his handling of the situation, my friend still had to accept the responsibility for the loss of profits.

A reputation for fulfillment of all
promises as well as a stability of character
that inspires confidence.

8.

RELIABILITY

Along with the willingness to accept responsibility for
the actions of those through whom he is working, another
"ethic" or principle of a good manager is that of reliability
or what might be called "future honesty."

This "future" honesty is a little more difficult to attain
than "present" honesty and is one of the ethics or principles
included here. "Don't make promises you can't keep," is
the theme of one section of a motion picture film on good
supervision. A good supervisor or manager is reliable.
What he says can be depended upon. He does not make
promises to his men he does not intend to fulfill. Neither
does he make promises to his boss he doesn't intend to
fulfill. Now the easiest way to avoid this problem is just
not to make any promises. But that is not what is meant
by reliability. In any organizational system it is necessary
daily to make many promises both up and down the line —
and to those on the same level as well as those outside the
organization. If you try to avoid this, you will fail miserably
in carrying out your job. Commitments from you are
necessary to permit others to carry out their functions just
as commitments from them are necessary for you to do
your job. Promises just cannot be avoided. But they can
be kept realistic. And when the pressure is put on to
make a better promise, make a better one *only* if you are
reasonably certain that you, too, can make it a reliable
promise.

Another area of reliability that gets many managers into

trouble is in reporting "facts" to your boss. These you have obtained from another source — and you have not been able to check them out or their reliability is questionable. If you are a reliable manager, your boss expects to be able to rely on you and make decisions on the basis of what you tell him. If it later turns out to be wrong, you alone are responsible as far as he is concerned. He doesn't blame the person who gave you the information; he blames you for not having your information verified before you gave it to him.

This does not seem fair, of course, but like accountability, it is part of the system of management that you must accept if you want to manage. The only way this problem can be overcome is to assure yourself that those on whom you rely are really reliable. Your careful selection of employees and your insistence on the honesty and reliability of others is obviously critical to your own reliability.

One of the most serious arguments I ever had with my dad was on just this point. I was General Manager of one of our plants at the time and something had failed on one of the new construction machines we were testing. Dad had asked me to find out what happened and why. I sent my plant superintendent scurrying for the answer and meanwhile, dad went straight to the operator of the machine, going around five levels in the organization, which as the boss it was his privilege to do (and which he frequently did). When I brought my answer to him, it didn't agree with the answer he had received. My reliability through the levels of the organization had broken down. I was immediately more concerned that my reliability through channels had broken down and he was more concerned about why I hadn't circumvented channels (as he did) to find out about his machine. Hence the heated discussion followed. We were both right, of course. The reliability factor *must* be there and a manager must *insist* that it be there. But at the same time a manager must frequently monitor this reliability directly to assure he won't become unreliable as I had done.

But your reliability as a manager extends to a broader area than just the promises you make or the information you convey. It also extends into your own character and habits as well. Both your employees and your boss should be able to rely on things you do not say as well as what you do say. They should be able to say, when they hear a rumor or are asked a question, that it is not true or my boss would have told me. And your boss should be able to rely on you so completely he knows he will get no "surprises" at the end of the month or at the end of the year in financial adjustments or other areas that could adversely affect the business. He should be confident that you are on your toes and that as soon as you become aware of something adverse you will let him know immediately so that he can adjust his own planning.

Reliability also includes movements and habits. It means both your boss and your employees knowing what to expect from you under certain circumstances. They need to know that your reaction to a difficult situation will not depend on what you ate for breakfast or what problems you may have at home. They need to know that you have a reliable pattern of reactions and behavior and will be consistent in it. This does not mean you cannot be disturbed and even visibly upset when something goes wrong, but it does mean that your degree of anger must be related to the degree of the problem and not to other variable factors. In other words, those with whom you work should be able to predict accurately the degree of anger or your specific reaction to a problem because that is the way you always react in a similar set of circumstances. That is, they can rely on your reactions. R. G. used to say, "It never pays to *get* mad, but sometimes it pays to *act* mad. The only trouble is my men say they aren't always sure that I'm just acting."

Reliability is, therefore, a principle that encompasses words, deeds, habits and reactions and which becomes an essential part of the code of ethics of a really good manager.

The ability to maintain a stance and a calmness, even in periods of flexibility and change, that inspires confidence and security in your team.

STABILITY

Stability is somewhat akin to reliability and yet it is different. It involves the ability to convey to those individuals with whom you work, both on your own level and those who work for you, an attitude, normally without words, that inspires confidence. People need to know that you know what you are doing and that any difficulties present can be overcome. This concept of stability may seem to be contrary to other characteristics dealt with in this book, but really it is not. It deals primarily with your attitude or stance during a difficult period of problems or change, and deals with the degree to which you, yourself, do not permit discouragement and instability to show through you to your people.

I have always enjoyed working with a person to whom there are no problems, just opportunities to gain more experience and to come up with new solutions. Life is made up of challenges which can be stepping stones to us to gain new insights, new levels of attainment and opportunities to tackle new problems. But to many, such a challenge becomes a stumbling block, a disrupting of the status quo, an extra burden or just something to complain about. It becomes almost purely an attitude concerning your outlook on life.

Attitudes are difficult to conceal and yet, to be stable, you must be able to do just that when you become discouraged and problems begin to get you down. Of course, the perfect way to conceal such an attitude is just not to allow yourself that natural tendency to become discouraged. Even though you do not say a word, others can read you from your facial expressions, your actions, and what you do not say or questions you do not or cannot answer. You might think you are concealing something when the truth is obvious to everyone around you.

Instability is contagious, mighty contagious. When you as a manager begin to appear unstable, or through your expression and actions appear worried, then those working for you will immediately become unstable and worried. And because they may not know why, they will think the worst and imagine things that may be a great deal worse than the actual situation. In this frame of mind their effectiveness in their job drops to a fraction of normal and the situation begins to snowball. The patriarch Moses recognized this concept when he addressed the people of Israel just prior to their entry into the promised land. He said regarding men going into battle, "What man is there that is fearful and fainthearted? Let him go return unto his house, lest his brethren's heart faint as well as his heart" (Deut. 20:8).

A good manager will level with his employees (to the degree that he is able to do so) and then exhibit an attitude of stability on his own part that will let them know beyond the shadow of a doubt that he is not concerned about the final outcome and will stay in there pitching all the way.

Part Four

PERSONALITY RELATED QUALITIES

With this section or group of qualities, we begin to deal more with the manager himself apart from the way he functions in his job. That is, we are looking at the personality characteristics, natural or acquired (and they can be acquired) that are helpful and often essential to becoming a good manager or leader.

As sons frequently attempt to imitate a father and even unconsciously adopt many of his traits, beliefs and attitudes, the same is true of a manager-employee relationship. Whether you want this to happen or not, you will often find that the people through whom you are attempting to get the job done will exhibit some of the same personality characteristics you exhibit. This point has just been emphasized in the previous chapter on stability. If these personality traits are good, then these good characteristics in your people will help you get the job done better, faster, more profitably and at less expense. On the other hand, if they are not good, the effects multiply in the other direction, and you will find it increasingly difficult to accomplish your goals.

These characteristics are not only inheritable and learned from the boss, they are even highly contagious. A smile immediately begets a smile, a frown begets a frown, and a worried look causes others immediately to start worrying. It works both ways and the results are almost immediate.

Thus, if you have complete control of your own personality, you can, to a large degree, control the personalities of the people working with you. The results are amazing, almost unbelievable.

If you are excited and enthusiastic about your work, you will create enthusiasm in your staff. If you are sensitive to situations and problems around you and yet do not over-react, but control your emotions, you will find that those working with you will learn to do the same. And, if you recover quickly from mistakes, problems or misfortunes, you will find you have put new values into the minds of your people as well.

Creating the climate within which people can work happily and productively without emotional upheavals is, after all, a significant part of getting the job done through people.

The possession of a contagious enthusiasm for the job, the product, or service of the company and the people who produce it.

10.

EXCITE-ABILITY

Just as instability is contagious negatively, so enthusiasm is contagious in the opposite direction. The genuine enthusiasm of a person can seldom be ignored by those working around him. Nothing makes a job easier and more enjoyable than being sold on what you are doing and the company or organization for whom you are doing it. And the excite-ability being discussed in this chapter is not excitement just for the sake of excitement, or that kind of excitement which occurs only when something big happens or something goes wrong. It is the capability to become excited about your job and your company in a real and genuine way. It is that sustained excitement or enthusiasm along with an energetic drive that motivates others around you.

Enthusiasm and drive are a necessary element in a successful individual's business career. And individuals are what make a company or an organization go. No organization can grow and progress without an enthusiastic team of managers and supervisors. For some of us, enthusiasm comes naturally; for others it must be cultivated and nurtured daily until it becomes a natural way of life. Even introverts can build personality, enthusiasm and drive where it does not exist naturally and biologically. But to do so requires an intense desire and an attitude that it can be done.

The manager of one of our factories has, through the

years, been one of these enthusiastic, excitable individuals with whom it is a pleasure to work. No problem or no job will get a negative response from him. It's always "If that's what you want done, we'll figure out a way to do it." When he tackled a job that way he usually did it. What's more, this same attitude infiltrated his entire organization. There was just no "It can't be done" philosophy at any level.

Now, of course, a good manager can't be reckless in such promises because he still must produce the goods. But it is always easier to put a harness on an excite-able manager than it is to build a fire under a discouraged one.

Recently a surge of orders came through to this particular plant after a "long dry spell." Our sales people soon became concerned that perhaps the plant couldn't produce all the units they were getting. This manager's retort was always, "Don't worry about the mules, just load the wagon!" Eventually a limit was reached and we had to back off on the orders, but nothing spurs on an organization like an executive who is enthusiastic about his product, his people and their ability to get the job done.

Any organization with whom you become identified has the right to expect you to give high priority to this enthusiasm. If enthusiasm is not natural to your personality, make a sincere effort to develop it. The organization's progress and success in meeting its goals and objectives will be largely in direct proportion to the degree you can inspire the entire organization with your enthusiasm and confidence for the future. Thus it has been with the manager I have described.

Motivating a group of people is sometimes difficult. Motivation cannot be created simply by following a set of rules or conditions, just as a good manager cannot become successful simply by following a set of rules or a pattern of behavior. Motivation is a characteristic which develops spontaneously when the proper conditions, circumstances and attitudes are present. One of the main conditions or attitudes that contribute to this motivation is the enthusiasm and drive of you, the manager.

Next to his genius and trust in God, perhaps the strongest factor in the building of a hard-working, loyal team by R. G. LeTourneau, was his undying enthusiasm and drive. From early morning until late at night (and he was never content to sit at a desk), he inspired his men with the excitement which he brought to any task before him. When men see that the boss is interested and excited (not just driving them, but genuinely excited about the outcome and the future,) they can't help but say that if the boss himself is that excited and enthusiastic it must be really great and there must be wonderful things ahead. With that they get excited, too, and the work progresses much faster than its normal rate.

And this same factor applies to any organization, and to any job to be done. Excitement and enthusiasm by the manager for the project or duties he has before him is extremely contagious to those around him and will in turn contribute greatly to the motivation of everyone and the success of the manager himself.

The ability to react, or refrain from
reacting, to situations, and a sensitivity
to the need for action
rather than reaction or passivity.

II.

REACT-ABILITY

Our actions toward others are an important part of our personality. The way we act toward other people is determined by our attitude toward them. This attitude is generally determined, in turn, by their actions toward us. This can, and frequently does, turn into a chain reaction which results in either of two extremes — a fight or jubilation. In other words, our actions toward others are, more often than not, reactions rather than actions. And when you react, you are really not in control of your actions. It's just as simple as that. Have you ever, when in a real good mood, had someone snap at you about something? What did you do? Most likely, you snapped right back. If you did, you were not in control of your actions. You let the other person determine your action by reacting to the way he acted rather than acting according to your better judgment.

The same procedure works in the other direction and can be used to your advantage. The other day I was having my car filled with gas. I noticed that the left front tire was going flat. After the attendant had finished filling the tank, I moved the car around to the service bay so he could fix the tire. The station manager said something to the atten-

dant which I did not hear. At this point the attendant began cursing and going about his work in a belligerent and
somewhat careless manner. He was upset! In fact, he was
mad!

Seeing the situation, I decided to experiment. I first tried
to engage the attendant in conversation with some sympathetic remarks about how difficult and irritating his job
must be at times. At first his response was gruff. But after
a few exchanges, which I kept pleasant from my side in
spite of his gruff replies he brightened up considerably.
Even when he had trouble getting the hub cap back on,
it did not disturb him because I sympathized with him
again by saying, "They surely don't think of you fellows
who have to put those things on when they design them,
do they?"

When the job was finished (and I know that I got a
much better job than it had earlier appeared I was going
to get), he was in a much better mood, and I'm sure he
thought I was a pretty nice guy. What he did was react
to my pleasant and sympathetic remarks even though he
was in a foul mood to start with.

This is the way of human nature and you can just about
depend on it. Unless a person realizes this phenomenon
and forces himself to act rather than react, you can get
the same results every time. If you get upset and cross, the
person you are talking to will do likewise even though he
may not have been that way to begin with. And if you
are pleasant and courteous, he will also become pleasant
and courteous just as the service station attendant did.
Sales persons and those who must deal with the public
are carefully trained not to react to an upset customer.
By a pleasant and agreeable disposition they can frequently
turn the customer's disposition around to an agreeable attitude.

An educational film produced some years ago pointed
this out very vividly. The plot line follows a man through
a day in his life where everything goes wrong for him and

he reacts to every situation making it worse. Then he is permitted the opportunity of living that day over again with some instructions on how to get along with people. The second time around the same things go wrong but this time he controls his reactions and turns every event into a pleasant experience and in the end has a wonderful day. It's just a story, but it vividly portrays what can actually happen when you act instead of react.

In addition to the need for action rather than reaction, there is also a need for action rather than inaction or passivity. I have seen many otherwise good managers who just could not get moving or take action on things. They were always studying the situation and analyzing, and when the action came it was too little or too late. Studying and analyzing are fine, and to be able to do them well is an admirable trait, but there is a fine line sometimes between this and just plain foot-dragging.

A close friend of mine, now retired, was never really able to get anywhere as far as leadership is concerned because he could not make decisions and consequently failed to act. He is intelligent, has a wonderful personality, loves people, and has helped thousands of people during his lifetime, but he just could not make those decisions that would have been necessary to make his own career more meaningful.

R. G. said frequently, "Show me a kid who never gets into trouble and I'll show you a kid who will never amount to anything." This may seem shocking at first. My father was not, however, trying to relate the "trouble making" to accomplishment. He *was* saying that unless a child has this drive or propensity for action in his life, he'll not go far. It's this drive and action that usually gets him into trouble. The "trouble" is then just an outward manifestation of this personality characteristic. It may be the manifestation of other characteristics, too. But if the child with this drive is channelled in the right direction, he usually becomes a real leader in life.

Do you act or react? This was the title of a *Reader's Digest* article several years ago. And to this I would add, "Do you act or inact?" This ability to control actions, reactions and inactions is certainly a vital personality characteristic required in becoming a good manager.

The ability to recover from mistakes or misfortunes (of yourself or others) with sufficient rapidity so as not to compound errors by dwelling on the past.

12.

RECOVER-ABILITY

We have talked a great deal about action and reaction and quite frequently we hear discussion about "reaction time." In driving a car or in certain dangerous occupations, reaction time can be vitally important. But what about your "recovery time"? Have you ever thought of that? Did you know that the recovery time of individuals varies many times more than does reaction time? I'm not talking about physical recovery after an illness or an accident. I'm talking about mental or psychological recovery after a tragedy, misfortune, or even after a chewing-out from the boss. How fast do you return to a stable state of mind?

Many people practically never recover after the death of a loved one. That death may drag them down psychologically for years or even for a lifetime. Others recognize that life must go on, and they regain their equilibrium quickly in a matter of hours or days. This does not mean necessarily that in one case the departed one was more loved or closer than in the other case, although that could be. However, it definitely could indicate that one has a slower recovery time than the other.

This applies to everyday business life as well. There are many things that happen in the course of a day or a week to set us back and cause us to lose efficiency in our job. This is normal and in some cases we just cannot prevent certain things from affecting us and our job. When it does happen, however, we can minimize the effect on us personally and on the people with whom we work by developing a quick recovery time.

An executive with whom I worked very closely for several years was an excellent man in his job. He knew it forward and backward and was able to accomplish a great deal. Normally he was a very enthusiastic person. He was sold on the organization and the people he worked with and except for one problem, he conveyed this enthusiasm well to others. Most people who worked very closely with him, however, felt he was "moody." And I guess this was the way it appeared. He would have his good days and his bad days. When he was up, he was great, but when he was down he was transparently down and everyone knew it. This was probably the one thing that kept him from reaching the top in his profession.

In attempting to analyze his behavior, I have come to the conclusion that he was not a "moody" man. He just had a slow recovery time. He had had many disappointments in his family, and he worked with people who would frequently "get to" him, making him frustrated. Instead of accepting these problems, however, and after handling each case as best he could, recovering his way back to normal enthusiasm, he would dwell on his difficulties. He would think about them, brood over them and talk to people about them, to the point that it took him a long time to recover. As a result, he appeared to be "moody" and unpredictable at times.

When someone criticizes you, are you upset for days or weeks? Does a minor accident make you jittery in your driving for months? When you lost that big order, did it take you several days to recover your selling steam? That is what I'm talking about. How fast can you analyze the situation, make decisions and correct it, and then look to the future without continuing to dwell on that past problem?

Dwelling on the past can create real problems. You, as a manager, should obviously benefit from past experiences and use them as guides for the future. A child learning to walk falls many times and gets right up to try again. Likewise you should also profit from past experiences, but you should never let the falling or failing experience leave you sitting on the floor.

The ability to recover rapidly from mistakes and unpleasant situations is a personality characteristic that is extremely valuable to you as a manager and leader.

Part Five

SELF RELATED QUALITIES

The previous section dealt with the more evident outward personality characteristics. This one will probe still deeper into your inner man. These characteristics may not be so obvious to those with whom you have daily contact but will, nevertheless, have a strong bearing on your future and overall capability as a leader and as a manager.

This fifth of the seven parts of this book deals with qualities which are strictly personal or attitude related. It is assumed that you have a real desire or thirst for more knowledge in management or else you would not be spending your time in reading this book or attempting to understand its contents. This, of course, is essential. Along with the desire for improvement (and the action tacked on to that desire which you have exhibited by the actual reading of the book), your attitudes toward yourself and the relationships of self to all of the facets of management are very important. This section deals with these basic attitudes concerning your personal or self relationship to management.

It is difficult, extremely difficult, for any of us to examine ourselves in terms of these inner qualities. Are they present? To what degree? And are they really there or do I just think they are? Can a person truly be objective about his own self-examination? On the other hand, can you really conduct a self-examination as to your objectivity? This all sounds confusing, doesn't it? That is why this section is one of the most difficult to apply.

As a real leader you must not only have control of your own personality but must, in addition, be able to evaluate and control your inner forces in such a way that they do not betray you in your efforts to get the job done through people.

The ability to set sound personal and
organizational goals compatible with
good leadership and good management.

13.

OBJECTIVE - ABILITY

Objectivity is several things. On one hand, it is being realistic and recognizing things as they really are rather than the way you would prefer them to be. It is also being sufficiently practical in your planning so that events, theoretically possible, do not unduly influence you. It is being specific rather than vague in orientation or direction. And it is being unemotional, attempting to view situations from the viewpoints of others rather than through your own prejudices. Probably the greatest enemies of objectivity are the two-fold twins of emotion and tradition.

Emotion plays a larger part in this than you might normally think. You see, your emotions are not really emotions to you. You will almost always classify them as experiences and values. It is only when the other fellow shows an extreme emotional bias that you really recognize it as emotion. And when a person lets his emotions overrule his objectivity, not only is he normally unaware that this is taking place but anyone who tries to point it out to him will be accused of being emotional instead. The best way I can explain this relationship of emotion to objectivity is to put it into the framework of what I call "relativity of importance."

This is the phenomenon of human nature that causes us to give a higher priority of time and attention to the things we like to do or in which we have this emotional involvement. If you like to fish, fishing can consume a great deal of your time and attention. The same is true of golf or any hobby you might develop. You are involved in it. You talk about it. You plan it, and it takes an inordinate amount of your time and effort. What really happens is that you become emotionally orientated in that direction. When this happens, you become less objective in the time your job requires or you spend with your family, etc. This is because your relativity of importance has become distorted. We concentrate on things emotional to us without any real regard to the relative importance of these things.

In management it is extremely important that our "relativity of importance" scale works accurately. We must determine the relative importance of the projects or tasks before us so as to budget our time and effort to these items according to their importance or value to the organization, rather than according to our system of emotional preference. This is being objective.

This relativity of importance concept also means the necessity of delegating to subordinates duties that are of relative unimportance to the overall organizational welfare. You must do this even though you become irritated that things are not being done your way — and even if these duties are in your special field of knowledge in which your subordinate may be less competent. Your time is more valuable and should be spent on more important things. This is a difficult decision to reach, but it is being objective.

A financial officer who becomes president of his company will find it difficult to give the needed attention to manufacturing, sales, service or other non-finance activities. He will be tempted to devote a great deal of time to minor details and "nit-picking" in the financial area. He finds it extremely difficult to delegate certain tasks to others because they won't do it exactly the way he wants it done (and to do it just that way may not *really* be important). Or he may feel he can do it better and faster than anyone else. What has happened? He is being emotional, not objective, and has let his relativity of importance become unbalanced.

Tradition, which really is just emotion that has a more specific time reference, is also a great enemy of objectivity. Not all traditions are bad, certainly. Traditions are often what give an organization its distinctiveness and care should be taken to properly evaluate tradition in the light of the character of the organization. Don't just discard it without analysis. But many times tradition becomes the excuse of a lazy mind for not coming up with a new and better way of doing things.

Another phase of objectivity which a good manager needs to develop carefully concerns the setting of goals and planning for the future. Maintaining objectivity here can also be difficult. We need to set our sights high enough to force us into action and a pattern of discipline, yet these goals need to be attainable in order to be objective.

In our company, we often accused my father of not being very objective or realistic when he estimated the cost of a new machine he wanted to build or the time required to build it. Generally, it would cost two or three times his estimate and would take two or three times the length of time to build it. What he was really doing was setting goals for us to shoot at, on the premise that if we thought we could do it in that length of time and at that cost, we would certainly come closer than we would have otherwise. This did not always work, however, because his goals were sometimes so unrealistic they were unreasonable and, therefore, really not objective. Whenever we would trap him in an obviously exaggerated situation of this type (when we all knew that he was making it a great deal better, or worse than it really was), he had a favorite saying that would always get him off the hook. He would tell us, "I'm just blowing it up a bit so you can see it better."

Obviously, there are times and occasions for goal-setting that may be a little far out. But the manager must make certain that this type of goal-setting does not cause him to be unrealistic in related operations. For example, you might convince your salesmen they can sell twice as much of your product next year, but unless you *know* they can and are really objective in analyzing the market, you had better not double the capacity of your plant. If you do, you are in trouble. It works the other way, too. You may demand that your manufacturing people produce twice as much next year, but you had better not let your salesmen take orders for twice as much unless you are sure it can actually be produced.

So, in your personal affairs, in controlling emotion and tradition, and in your organizational priorities and planning, make sure that you are objective in your attitude and analyses if you want to be a really good manager.

would be almost a dichotomy in that it involves an attitude of non-self-aggrandizement and at the same time leaves room for an active and dynamic personality. A more appropriate term might be the "capacity for self-dispensability." Let me explain further by example.

The Apostle Peter, probably the least "humble" and the most impulsive of all apostles in the Bible, had just performed a miracle of healing on a lame man in the temple at Jerusalem. A gaping crowd surrounded him. "Men of Israel," he said, "What is so surprising about this? And why look at us as though we by our own power and godliness had made this man walk?"

If we were to perform such a miracle today, we would be looking over our shoulder to see if the TV cameras were rolling and if the wire services had the whole story on us. But Peter said, in effect, "What are you looking at us for? We didn't do anything. It was the Lord who did it!" Now Peter was not weak or pious. He was a vibrant, active individual. Yet he had this capacity to do a disappearing act as far as self was concerned.

These is another example of this in the Bible. Moses, after spending forty days on the mountain talking to God, came down with his face glowing. But we are told that he had an "unawareness" that his face shone. He had the glow of God on his face but kept his self-consciousness of this at a zero level (Exod. 34:29).

My father, Mr. R. G. LeTourneau, was probably the greatest living example of this characteristic I ever knew. He had this vibrant dual personality. He accomplished astounding things in his lifetime and had every reason to be proud. Yet without being weak or pious, he took no credit for himself. He gave all the credit to God. If you had known him in his home life as I did, you would agree he had complete self-dispensability or disappearance in all human or natural aspects. He would say, "You can only sleep in one bed at a time. You can only wear one suit of clothes at a time. And I know you can't eat any more than I can." His life was almost just that simple in

his self needs, yet he literally changed the face of the earth
with his construction machinery and with his successful
relating of Christianity to business operations.

The second facet of replace-ability is somewhat similar
to the first, although it moves in another direction. This
principle holds that wherever possible you should acknowl-
edge the contribution others have made (even for things
you might normally be credited with, or things that the
other person does not actually deserve credit for). This
doesn't sound reasonable but let me explain further. A
manager must get the job done through people. The greatest
skill a manager can attain is that of being able to gather
around himself such people as will get the job done. This
means that you shouldn't be looking for credit for getting
the job done, but for credit for surrounding yourself with
people who can get the job done.

The greatest compliment I could receive from my dad
was for him to tell someone, "Rich knows how to gather
people around him who can get the job done." That is a
much greater compliment to a manager than being told
that he himself is doing a good job.

So giving your subordinates credit for doing a specific
job well is actually more complimentary to you than if you
had received the credit yourself. Besides this, your willingness to give them the credit will motivate your people more
than anything else you can do. On the other hand, the
manager who is disliked the most is the one who takes the
accomplishments of his people and represents them as his
own. Even if he does this unintentionally, it can be devastating to the morale and motivation of his subordinates.

I feel that this next point is the ultimate degree to which
you can motivate people to action. This involves taking
an idea, whether it is yours or another's, and then con-
vincing your co-worker, be he a subordinate or a superior,
that it is his idea, not yours. He will become very enthusiastic about something he feels is his idea because he has
identified himself with it. We have already said you should
be more interested in getting the job done than in getting

credit for it. Thus, if you can get him enthused about it by making him think it was his idea, you really come out the winner.

Several years ago I had covered this concept of "making someone else think it's his idea," in a college course I was teaching on Human Relations. In my class was a very personable young man who, with some other students, had leased and was operating a service station near the campus. One day he came to class very excited and told me, "It works! It works!" He then went on to explain what had happened.

He had been trying to sell oil changes by pointing out to the motorist that his oil was dirty and needed changing — all without much success. After hearing this concept that if you can make someone think something is his idea instead of yours, he will be much more apt to buy it, the student had a bright idea.

He would pull the oil stick, and if the oil looked dirty he would bring the stick around to the driver's window. Holding the stick in one hand, he would run his finger in the oil and turn the finger up so the motorist could see it. (Oil looks even dirtier against a flesh colored finger than it does on the stick). All this he would do without saying a word. More often than not, the motorist was almost forced to say, "That oil's kinda dirty, isn't it? I must be due for a change. Can you change it for me right now?" Of course the answer was, "Yes sir!" with a smile. What he was doing was instead of telling the man his oil was dirty (the attendant's idea), he was forcing the motorist to make that conclusion himself. Then it was the motorist's idea and he was ready to act on it.

The student then went on to tell me he had sold quite a number of oil changes that way the day before. Previously he had been having little success. So it does work. Give someone else the credit. Make him think it is his idea and he'll really go for it.

The third facet of replace-abiilty is recognizing the need to train a replacement for yourself. It is only as you invest your knowledge and talents in others and create in them the capability to do your job, that you, yourself, can advance to a higher position, or be able to say that your special talents will be perpetuated after you have gone. Many times I needed a man for a particular management position and had to pass over the otherwise best qualified man because he was too valuable where he was and had no replacement or number two man who could take over his job. Taking a less qualified man for the promotion is many times less harmful overall to the organization than taking the best man and leaving a key spot without anyone who can handle it. It's a shame that this happens, but it does, time and again. If you really want that job up the line, just make sure you have a lieutenant well trained and ready to step into your shoes or you might just get passed by.

Replace-ability? Yes, it is important, for your own satisfaction, well-being, job-satisfaction, and advancement.

Part Six

BALANCE RELATED QUALITIES

Having progressed through the job, the people, the principles, the personality of the manager, and the inner self of the manager, I would like to embark on another important area. This involves the combining of some of the various characteristics set forth previously, especially where there is a seeming conflict between them. In effect this will become a tightrope walk as we move through this sixth set of qualities presented here.

The analogy of the tightrope is a good one here. The balance required between these qualities is difficult and delicate and those who have not spent much time and concentration on balancing their "people" skills will discover a strong tendency to fall off on one side or the other.

Balance, and the judgment that it takes to keep all situations in equilibrium, is the common thread that ties together many of the preceding elements where they seem to be in conflict. It is almost like the tightrope walker who carries with him a long bar. You might say he has enough trouble staying up there without carrying that huge bar, and that carrying the bar is in conflict with his being able to walk on the tightrope. But when you understand fully just why he's carrying the bar and how it actually helps him to stay up there (not hinders him), then you can see the compatibility and necessity of the combination. So it is with many of the elements in this book. They may seem incompatible, but when you really understand how they work together and why they are there, it will be much clearer to you why they are needed and how they actually help each other, not hinder.

Since balance is the key to this section, and because it is so critical, the concept of balance (what it is, how it functions and why it is necessary) will be discussed first.

There are many kinds of balance all of which are important in their own way. The balance of the "balance wheel" in your wrist watch is critical to its keeping accurate time. The balance of the flywheel in your car engine keeps it from flying apart at high speeds. Proper balance of your tires keeps them from shaking the car badly beyond a certain speed. A gyro compass depends critically on the balance of its gyro to point an accurate compass heading to the ship's captain or to the aircraft pilot. Many more examples could be given but it is sufficient to say that the physical balance within an instrument or mechanism can be extremely important.

In the biological realm balance also plays an important role. Our diet must be properly balanced in terms of the food we eat. It must also be balanced in terms of total intake (calories) as against our total physical output. An imbalance will cause us either to gain or lose weight. This is also true with respect to activity and rest. Our bodies have one of the most critical thermostats known to man when it comes to balancing heat and cold. Much of medical science today is concerned with just this facet of maintaining a balance in the systems of our bodies.

In family situations, which in many ways are similar to the management concepts presented here, balance also plays an important role. There must be "give and take" for a family to live and operate harmoniously together. This is why so many families and homes are disrupted in our society — the inability to create a balance in the home. Children must be loved but they must also be disciplined, and it's the balance between these that is critical. All one without the other will destroy the child. Parents must also balance their time between work and recreation. They also need to spend time together as a couple for a happy and harmonious marriage.

In education, balance again shows itself as a critical issue. Balance in the type of courses taken is important in the development of a well-rounded individual. An equilibrium between the theory presented and a practical application of that theory is also important. Too much of one or the other will not produce the well educated and adjusted person who is so greatly needed in our society. The same is true of the needed balance between mere head knowledge and the character building aspects of education. A truly balanced education is well distributed around the academic theory, the practical application of it, and a broad "purpose-in-life" orientation which includes character building and religious foundations.

As is evident in almost any aspect of life or activity, the matter of proper proportioning or weighing of the various extremes and orientations available is extremely important. So it is also in a business situation and particularly as it relates to management and the application of the principles outlined in this book. Just as balance can be very important to the stability of an organization, extremism can be equally as damaging. A program of extreme austerity can damage the long-range growth and well-being of a company. On the other hand, orientation of affluency can be detrimental to current profits and the resultant growth potential. The same is true with respect to a strong marketing orientation without market development. Long-range planning vs. sensitivity to current problems and efficiency is another area requiring a delicate balance.

In management generally, and in the handling of functions and people particularly, this matter of balance looms even more critically. In a business or management situation we must have controlled emotions. And while making full use of our intuitive judgment, we must let facts and experience (rather than emotions) control decisions. This need not destroy one's individuality or personality but actually should make better use of it by subduing natural human tendencies toward extremism.

In the discussions to follow I will attempt to relate the three elements of our human make-up: the intellect (head), the physical activity (hands), and the emotion (heart). The three areas of balance between each pair of these aspects will illustrate quite well the necessity of balance in management and in dealing with people.

The ability to be both understanding and
yielding, particularly on trivial things which
have little real importance, but which may be
very important to someone else, yet — be tough,
persistent and unyielding on important items
where profits, growth and overall impact may be in
danger, and — to keep personal emotions from im-
pairing your ability to discern between the two.

16.

TOUGHNESS AND
UNDERSTANDING

(Head and Heart)

This element occurs more frequently and is probably the
most difficult for the average person to reconcile of the
three facets of balance to be discussed. It involves this
matter of how, or when, to be tough (and even difficult)
in your dealing with people as opposed to how and when
to have compassion and understanding for them. Being
tough or understanding is generally not difficult. And many
people are consistently either one or the other. But good
management requires that you be *both*. And on occasion
it may be necessary to be both at the same time! Impossible? No, it is entirely possible. And the manager who
has mastered this skill has really come a long way in his
people-handling ability.

As with all of the combinations of balance discussed in
this part of the book, we are not talking about being a
compromiser or a middle-of-the-roader. We are talking
about how to exercise judgment in knowing when to be

tough, I mean really tough, and when to be understanding and really "soft-hearted" toward the people with whom you work. There are instances when being too lenient would destroy the discipline and efficiency of the organization. Then there are also occasions when being too tough would do exactly the same thing. You must have a sensitivity for which to be in every instance. How do you determine this? It appears to be an impossible task, doesn't it? But it's not really. There are some fundamentals that if properly applied will allow you to be tough when you need to be without creating a feeling of injustice among your people. If you can be lenient or understanding when it is possible, then when it is necessary for you to be tough, you will be properly understood. In other words, be understanding most of the time and when you have to be tough, be sure to have a good and understandable reason for it. Let me explain further.

In an earlier chapter, I used the term "relativity of importance." At the risk of being somewhat redundant, I would like to repeat something I said earlier but from this perspective of balance between toughness and understanding. This term deals with the proper use of time and efforts in producing the most results for your company. It also applies, however, to gaining the respect of your subordinates by demonstrating your non-emotion and non-prejudices, your fairness in all your dealings, to the point that they will have confidence in your ability to discern between toughness and understanding. Let's look at this relativity of importance again. Basically, it concerns itself with the assignment of our time to tasks that bear the highest level of importance to the well being of the organization. Our natural tendency is to assign priorities on the basis of what we like (or dislike) doing instead.

This tendency also creeps into our handling of people. If the matter before us awaiting a decision is one to which we have an emotional reaction (or if the person presenting it to us does so in a way that we react to him rather than the matter being presented), we tend to make our decision based on those emotions or reactions. In such a situation, we do not base it on what is best for the organization. The same can be true conversely. If the matter touches our emotions or if the person presenting it creates a favorable reaction, we tend to go along even if the decision is not best for the organization. This results in "politics" and favoritism and is generally apparent to everyone in the organization but ourselves. You think you have made the right decisions because you are looking at them through your own emotions and reactions. Operating in this manner, you will frequently be understanding when you should be tough and tough when you should be understanding. Then you are in trouble! How do you overcome this? Simple! Leave your emotions and reactions out! Here is a suggested failsafe procedure.

1. Analyze carefully the tasks, matters and decisions before you and determine the relative importance of each to the organization. On the basis of this scale assign your time and effort rather than according to your own emotional system of preferences.

2. Where the total tasks to be accomplished exceeds the time you have available for these tasks, delegate to your subordinates those things of lesser importance to overall company welfare. Do this even though it may cause you irritation to see things not being done your way, or even though your special field of knowledge makes you more competent than your subordinates.

3. Learn to be tougher when the matter being handled is of high importance to the organization and of low importance to the individual. Conversely, learn to be more understanding when the matter is of greater importance to the individual and less importance to the organization.

Following the above procedure will assure you the job will get done properly and that in doing so you will have created for yourself the maximum amount of respect.

People are not ignorant or stupid. Generally they can see through you when you let your emotions and preferences rule your decisions and handling of people. They can also recognize quickly when you are fair and just and when you have good reason for being tough. Delegating and conceding on the relatively unimportant matters also has a great value in the training of your subordinates. It gives them an opportunity to make decisions and carry out functions at a minimum risk to the organization.

So don't be a middle-of-the-roader. Be tough when it is necessary. Be understanding when you can. And above all, keep your own emotions and system of emotional preferences out of your evaluations.

The ability to maintain a balance between
the knowledge, the study and the theory that
are necessary, and the action that must be
initiated on this information to see a
project to its successful completion.

17.

KNOWLEDGE AND ACTION

(Head and Hands)

Our technological revolution and the knowledge explosion
has forced upon us a great urgency and necessity for
higher educational attainment by our youth and the popu-
lace in general. This emphasis on education and scientific
achievement is certainly valid and the results of it have
revolutionized may fields of endeavor, particularly the
aerospace industry and medicine. We are told now that the
amount of technical information available to us doubles
every ten years. That's four times as much now as we had
twenty years ago during the Korean War. We have available to us over 100,000 journals being produced to communicate this explosion of knowledge. These journals are
produced in more than sixty different languages around the
world. And we are also told that the number of these
journals will double every fifteen years. The advance of
such things as computer technology has enabled us to
store information, retrieve it, and make complex calculations. We can now conceive and build machinery and
structures impossible within the life span of any single
engineer or scientist previously. There is literally no end
to the astounding examples and illustrations which could
be cited as evidence of our knowledge explosion and its

value to society. But there are some dangers associated with this explosion as well.

We have become so enamored of the value of education and knowledge that we frequently let it unbalance our thinking. Indeed we begin to think this wonderful knowledge and technology as a panacea for all our ills. This is not the case. Certainly we should use what knowledge is available to us to the fullest extent, but we must do so with careful judgment and common sense. Many management personnel seem to feel, for example, that the computer is the answer to all their problems. They have been led to believe that if they can pose the proper questions, somehow the computer can come up with any and every answer. What many do not realize is that the information the computer has available to it was put there by a man, by its programmer. The computer has no resources except material fed into it and can give no answers except those attainable by mathematically analyzing or sorting out the information given it. There is absolutely no magic in it, only speed. It really can't even add two and two. It must add one, four times.

What I'm saying is, in our haste to unload our problems and decision making onto a machine, let's take a more practical approach by realizing the limitations in that machine as well as the responsibilities we have as a manager. I'm not deriding the computer or any other device. I'm just pointing out that each device has its limitations and a good manager will ascertain those limitations and act accordingly. Without the computer handling financial information and solving engineering and scientific equations, modern society would be thrown into chaos. But many companies are also thrown into chaos by jumping too quickly or too deeply into what they think the computer can do for them specifically.

But computers are only an example of what I want to illustrate in this chapter. They are not the real thrust of the problem. The basic problem is that so many of our new generation of highly educated managers seem to feel that "knowledge," per se, is all we need. They seem to feel that if this inexhaustible body of knowledge is within their grasp, they can automatically become good managers and solve all their problems. Regardless of the level of technical training or the level of sociological and psychological training a manager must have, there is more to it than that. Knowledge cannot take the place of experience and attitudes. Neither can it take the place of intuition or the "plus" characteristic to be explored later. The "practical" element, putting this knowledge into practice, is the key to its benefit to the field of management and to society as a whole. The ability of a manager (you) to take this body of knowledge, evaluate it properly, adjust it where necessary, apply it in the manner intended for it, and then act on it with enthusiasm and good judgment — this is what I mean by balance.

The man with knowledge only, without the experience and action to go with it, reminds me of two men who went into partnership together. As the story goes one man with the money and the other with experience joined together in business. After a period of time had passed, the one with the experience had the money and the one with the money had the experience!

Remember, balance is not a middle-of-the-road position or a wishy-washy approach to knowledge or action. Rather, it is a strong belief in wisdom and a thorough understanding of what it can and can't do for you, coupled with the action necessary to get the job done through your experience and judgment.

The ability to both mix and separate (the ethical, emotional and spiritual from) the physical business aspects of any given situation, recognizing the necessity of ethics and Christian principles in business, utilizing them to the fullest in the conduct of business, yet not allowing this concept to cause you to run a "soft'" business any more than you would let business concepts "harden'" your Christianity or ethics.

18.

ETHICS AND PROGRESS

(Heart and Hands)

This final discussion of the three combinations of balance present in stabilizing our intellect, actions and emotions, deals with the latter two, our actions and emotions. Thus I have titled this chapter — ethics and progress. The ethics aspect encompasses our emotions and the religious principles on which a business should be conducted, regardless of the religious orientation of its managers. The progress deals with getting the job done in a practical manner. Some construe this as an excuse for doing so at any and all cost as far as the ethics side is concerned.

No doubt, many businesses have succeeded with no regard for ethics or personal values. But this is the exception, not the rule. For any long-term growth, and the good public image that is necessary over the long pull, a sound ethical policy is mandatory. Our business society will not long tolerate the presence of such an unethical operation in its midst.

What many do not realize is that ethics and progress

are entirely compatible. Here again, I am not advocating a middle-of-the-road position that could be considered a compromise. Rather, I am calling for a dual position, strong beliefs on one side and a solid business-like operation on the other. The inability of many to comprehend the compatibility of the two was brought home to me very forcefully in an incident that happened several years ago.

R. G. LeTourneau, my father, was renowned as one of America's outstanding Christian businessmen and had built an outstanding manufacturing business from nothing. He was interested in a jungle development project in one of the smaller South American countries. This particular country had a need for a large volume of construction equipment and was interested in purchasing several pieces of this equipment from our company. At the time, I was involved in some of the negotiations between the Minister of Public Works of that country and our company management. I had made a special trip in our company plane to present what we thought was a fair exchange of machinery and privileges between us in the form of a proposed contract. At the appropriate time we were ushered into the Minister's office and after some pleasantries, he proceeded to read the proposed document which consisted of several pages. After a few minutes he finished and looked up at us, a puzzled expression on his face. With deep concern in his voice he said, "I thought Mr. LeTourneau was a religious man. This sounds like a businessman wrote it."

With those fifteen words he said without any equivocation exactly what many people wrongly believe – that you can't be a Christian and still be a good hard-nosed businessman. He had evidently counted heavily on the fact that we were a Christian organization and as such would be less than sharp in our business acumen. Thus he hoped to get a real bargain in the equipment he needed (the end result was that the whole deal was later called off). But rather than Christianity and good business being incompatible, just the opposite is true. Christian principles are absolutely essential in any business and business principles are a proper compliment to almost any phase of Christtianity. It is always profitable for them to be integrally related. You can balance them to fit a particular set of circumstances and perhaps lean a little one way or the other according to good judgment, but the two areas must be both kept in the picture and they must be in relative balance.

Being a hard-nosed businessman also includes the practical aspects discussed earlier. It means that the job must get done. Without this there will be no business and no opportunity to apply the social and moral values in which we believe. But the job must not get done at the expense of these values lest, when we arrive, there are no values to apply. In that case any successes we have achieved would be empty and void of personal satisfaction.

Part Seven

SPECIAL "PLUS" QUALITIES

There is more to management than the eighteen qualities we have discussed thus far, including the comprehensive ones on balance just concluded. Management is more than a rule book, more than a study of technology and human behavior. It is more than having certain experiences and a certain background. And certainly it is more than just being the son of the founder of the company (as it happened in my case). There is wisdom needed and required that bears little relationship to years or to position or to heritage. And it is this wisdom and judgment (or at least the free access to it), that I will attempt to explain as forthrightly as I know how in this seventh part of the book.

As I stated earlier, this section is really the reason for the existence of the entire book. It is its justification or rationale. Without this section, *Management "Plus"* would be just another book, and there are already hundreds of those. I hope we have been able in the preceding chapters to capture your thoughts and present in a readable and practical manner a sequence of elements that you may not have considered before. And perhaps in your mind this book is already justified. But not so in my mind.

There is more to life than just winning the game, or attaining a certain standard of living, or making a few bucks to leave to our heirs. Why are you striving? What happens to what you have accomplished thirty, forty or fifty years from now after you are gone? Will you have anything of real value left? What's more, where will you be? Have you ever given that matter any thought? Chances are you have. And probably some very serious thought at that. But what to do about it has undoubtedly been hazy in your mind. Religion is for women and preachers, right? Is this what has troubled you? You say Christianity just isn't compatible with a hard-nosed business career such as the one to which you have committed yourself. It just presents so many problems you can't reconcile yourself to the risk involved. If this is your problem, I have news for you.

Not only is Christianity compatible with business, it is the greatest thing that ever happened to a business or a business career! Talk to any businessman who is really an out-and-out Christian, one who has accepted Jesus Christ as his personal Savior and has dedicated his life, his career and his business to God. Ask him how he feels about it. There are thousands of men across the country who have done this and would have it no other way. Many of these have associated themselves together in "civic club" type organizations and have been instrumental in getting this message out to thousands of other businessmen around the country. They are successful in their work and live a fruit-ful, peaceful and harmonious life — because they have found the answer that most men in business are looking for. How many people have figuratively decided that a plunge at the seashore is undesirable because they have tested the water with their toes and have decided it's too cold to enjoy a good swim? I say, "Come on in, the water's fine!"

Let me explain all this in the following three chapters dealing with special "Plus" qualities in management. These are the elusive elements for which authors have searched unsuccessfully for decades (or at least they have not been able to reduce them to writing). In a way, they are not clearly definable. On the other hand they include one of the simplest and most elementary concepts present in today's complex society. If you have read this far, *don't leave me now*. We are ready to discuss the keys that unlock the mystery and make it so simple and so practical that no one, literally *no one*, with a desire to use them will find them unavailable. We are now ready to "put it all together." These then are the (1) Foundations and Purpose, the (2) Internal Guidance System, and the (3) Unexplainable, Undefinable Motivation that make management an attainable and enjoyable profession for all who will heed this message.

*Every man's career, his desire for success,
and his actions, are built on the concept of life
and the objectives toward which he is aiming. Some
are good, some are not so good, and there's a
surefire way of knowing which yours are.*

19

FOUNDATIONS AND PURPOSE

Our society, more than any before it in the history of civilization, is faced with rapid and even radical changes. In many cases it becomes necessary continually to re-evaluate everything before us in a new light. This constant change forces us to take a long, hard look at some of the traditions and foundations of society and examine their value and relationship to current problems and events. Someone has said that if you can stay calm in our present status of radical change and revolutionary technology, you're not a genius, you just don't know what's going on. In considering this matter of what are and what are not foundations and purpose on which we can build with confidence, let's first examine this matter of change and what it is doing and undoing for our society.

Recently in a national business magazine an economist stated that half the energy consumed by man in the past two thousand years, has been consumed in the last one hundred years. There has been more metal and materials extracted from mines since 1910 than was extracted in all history before that time. Another almost unbelievable fact has come to light: approximately twenty-five percent of the people who have ever lived on the face of the earth, are living today. Medical science has undergone some rather dramatic changes also. A few years ago it was estimated that ninety percent of the drugs prescribed today were unknown ten years previously. At that time it was calculated that three-fourths of those currently in use would be obsolete in another four years. Open heart surgery, heart transplants, delicate brain operations and the unlocking of the secrets of the brain in the RNA and DNA fluids are also developments of much significance. Educational patterns are changing rapidly, too, along with all of these other changes.

Just attempting to keep up with advancing technology is problem enough for education, but in addition to that, educators are going through enormous systems and methods changes themselves. The number of students attending college has doubled in the past eleven years and will increase another fifty percent in the next eight years.

Can we find a common thread that ties all this together? Yes, I believe we can. But first let's talk about general concepts that bridge all these areas, matters dealing with the meaning and importance of foundations.

Everyone recognizes the necessity of a proper foundation in the erection of a large building. The larger the building, the stronger must be the foundation. If it is a tall building or if it stands on poor soil the foundation must compensate by going down deeper into the earth. In addition, if the building is to withstand heavy stresses from the elements, such as high winds, hurricanes, etc., the foundation must compensate for that as well. This same concept can be utilized in examining many other fields of endeavor.

The computer, as we said earlier, is no magic machine. A computer merely speeds up the computation of basic mathematical calculations. It operates on some very basic foundational laws of mathematics. These laws must be maintained. If they are violated, the computer goes amuck. It must have this basic structure to operate successfully. The laws of thermodynamics with which we have been able to send a man to the moon have changed little in the past seventy-five years. We have learned to use them in a different light but the basic laws have always been there. They form a foundation for our space activities. To violate them even to a microscopic degree would cause the utter failure of a space mission. We can change and adjust the use of these laws but we cannot change the basic laws. The same is true in medicine. There are basic systems in the human body which must be maintained. Modern medical technology can perform miracles as long as it recognizes these basic foundational systems and builds its change and developments around them. Even in education there are certain foundations of character building and understanding of life which must be kept inviolate. Tampering with these values, on which the foundations of education must be built, is causing the major disruptions in our system today.

In the religious area also, we are facing much change. This is the common thread I would like to trace through all the previous discussions to give us something concrete and substantial, a personal foundation, if you please. What I have said previously in this book does not constitute the foundation on which you must build your life or career. They are instead, building blocks toward a purpose in life. Let me give you the formula for a solid foundation, one with which you can compare your own (you do have one, you know, be it good or not so good). This you can easily adopt if your own is inadequate to do the job.

Let me base what I have to say on the Bible, using this as the only source for developing our foundations. Regardless of what you might personally think of the Bible, it is the world's all time best seller. It has been translated into the greatest number of languages and has withstood the attacks of the most severe critics in history for centuries without weakening in the slightest. Its authenticity and its power grows steadily stronger with the years. Thus it cannot be ignored. What the Bible has to say must be confronted. The Bible itself recognizes that what it says must sound foolish to those who do not believe (1 Cor. 1:

18) but that it is in reality the power of God (Rom. 1:16). What does the Bible say about foundations?

In the *Living Bible* translation of the first letter to the Corinthian Christians, Paul deals with this matter of a foundation.

> God, in his kindness, has taught me how to be an expert builder. I have laid the foundation and Apollos has built on it. But he who builds on the foundation must be very careful. For no one can ever lay any other real foundation than that one we already have — Jesus Christ. But there are various kinds of materials that can be used to build on that foundation. Some use gold and silver and jewels; and some build with sticks, and hay, or even straw! There is going to come a time of testing at Christ's Judgment Day to see what kind of material each builder has used. Everyone's work will be put through the fire so that all can see whether or not it keeps its value, and what was really accomplished.

> Then every workman who has built on the foundation with the right materials, and whose work still stands, will get his pay. But if the house he has built burns up, he will have a great loss. He himself will be saved, but like a man escaping through a wall of flames (1 Cor. 3:10-15).

As you are undoubtedly quite aware, not everything in religion is built on the foundation which the apostle describes here. Not even all that is done in the name of Christianity and the church, sad to say, is built on this foundation. But like the basic laws of mathematics, thermodynamics, medicine, education, etc., there is also a basic law of life and living that must be observed to avoid a catastrophe. This foundation the apostle Paul clearly identifies as the person of Jesus Christ. And Christ Himself in response to "doubting" Thomas's question, ". . . how can we know the way?" said to him, "I am the Way — yes, and the Truth and the Life. No one can get to the Father except by means of me" (John 14:5, 6 *The Living Bible*).

The person of Jesus Christ then *is* the foundation. Our acceptance of that fact and our acceptance of Him personally as the intercessor between us and the Father is absolutely essential in providing the foundation necessary for a solid and unwavering life and career. Those things we do beyond this are, again, the building blocks for the structure of our life and career. As the apostle has said, we can use good building materials or poor ones and they will survive or not depending on which we use. But even though what we accomplish here on earth may be destroyed because we didn't use the right materials, if we have the foundation, it will survive and we ourselves will be saved through the Judgment Day. The foundation must be the first step, however. Our morals, our business ethics, our church attendance, our family life are all part of the building blocks or superstructure that is built on the foundation. If you already have this foundation in your life, great! Let's build on it properly through the concepts in the last two characteristics to be presented. If you don't have this foundation, you'll have to stop right here. Without it, you can't really build with the type of building blocks I'm talking about. You'll have to work out your own problems. The "plus" factor of this book is not available to you to use in your career. You'll just have to stumble through it the best you can.

But wait! You don't have to go that route unless you just *want* to do it the hard way. You *can* have the foundation I've been referring to. It has been offered to everyone just for the taking. There is one catch, however. You must personally accept it. God will not force it on anyone. If you don't want it, you don't have to take it. But if you do want it and will accept it of your own free will, it is available to you this very instant as you read these words. How? Find a Bible and read it for yourself. It's easy.

First, recognize that you're a sinner (we all are, we were born that way) (Rom. 3:23). Second, recognize that sinners deserve eventual death (Rom. 6:23). Third, recognize that God loved us to the extent that even though we are sinners and God can't look on sin, He sent His Son Jesus Christ to die in our place for our sin (Rom. 5:8).

Fourth, recognize that all we have to do to accept this sub-stitution God has provided. Call on God, believe what He has done, and confess to men that we have believed (Rom. 10:9, 10, 13).

Then all you have to do is *do* it. You don't need a preacher. You don't have to join a church (that can come later). Just recognize the four concepts above and believe that God will accept you, and He'll do it (John 1:12, 1 John 5:13). Then tell someone else about it and you're on your way. You then have the foundation. It's instantaneous. No waiting period, no delay. Then you can really begin to build something worthwhile in your life.

But this is not the end of my management book. It is really only the beginning. Because getting the foundation is just the first step. Now you can really use the principles I have set forth for you. And if you have difficulty with any of them, you have the power available to you in Christ to commandeer a new strength in an area where you may have had a weakness before. It's a whole new ball game. And it's great! Let's look further now into this exciting new life and what it can do for us beyond providing the foundation stones and giving us eternal life. Read on!

The possession of that special quality of judgment
that does not necessarily relate to theory or
experience; the development of, and reliance upon,
an internal guidance system that is separate and
distinct from knowledge and experience.
It may be called intuition, a sixth sense,
or it may be called supernatural guidance,
but it must be (and can be) there.

20.

INTERNAL GUIDANCE SYSTEM

Decision-making at the executive and managerial level is a topic which has been studied widely. There have been entire texts written on this subject alone. Naturally, decision-making is an area of extreme importance to the executive. It is in this area of making decisions that he rises or falls. How often is he correct or how often is he wrong?

How does the executive make critical decisions? There are many quantitative methods or guides available to most executives. The computer is used extensively for the gathering of masses of information on which to base critical decisions. On occasion the computer can be programmed even to analyze the information and present various numerical alternatives or even the best alternative to the manager. Various other techniques such as PERT (Program Evaluation and Review Technique), statistical analysis, systems analysis, linear programming, etc., are used along with the computer and sometimes without it to come up with a choice that seems best. But is this really the way major decisions are made?

Recently I read of a survey conducted in the West Coast aerospace industry regarding this matter of decision-making. And if any industry is thoroughly exposed to the above quantitative guides, it is this industry. Yet, the project managers questioned used subjective methods (experience, judgment, etc.) and just plain analysis six to one over the more sophisticated methods. In other words, the human brain and its ability to ". . . assemble all of the elements in a situation, assign intuitive weights to them, and come quickly to a satisfactory solution still surpasses rational models processed through a computer" (*Iron Age*, December 16, 1971, p. 29). This could be verified from many other sources as well. There are just too many factors to be considered in a major decision. These cannot be properly weighted and fed into the computer, or the quantitative formula, so that a manager can view its computed decision with enough confidence to risk his career and his company on it. So there is more to this matter of decision-making and guidance than a numerical evaluation,

There is also more to it than just applying the results of experience and the advice and counsel of others. Making decisions is a lonely matter. You will find many who are ready to offer advice and even a few (though not too many) who would also take the responsibility for the decision if you would allow them to make it. The problem is that you can't really give away the responsibility. It is still on your shoulders and since you are going to be responsible, you normally want to make the decision yourself. That's when you have to get alone with yourself, at least mentally, and face the issue alone. You use all the facts, experience and advice you can muster. Then you assign relative weights to all of this and come up with the decision. What you have done, however, is more than just a mental exercise. You have relied on something within you which gave you a "gut" feel: this was the way to go. Ask any top executive. If he is honest, he'll tell you that there is a certain amount of this "gut" feel in every decision he makes. And how sharp this sense is, how intuitive it is, many times will determine whether a man is successful or not in his career. Some have a knack for it, others just have the knack for making the wrong decisions.

You may call this what you like. You can describe it, as I have already, as "gut" feel. Or it can be called a real sensitive intuition. Some would prefer the term "sixth sense." And some might go so far as to call it ESP (Extra Sensory Perception). If you are a Christian, and if you have discovered the foundation in your life discussed in the previous chapter, you don't have to call it any of these things. In fact, you don't even have to guess what it is or wonder if it is reliable in your case. You can know what it is and its reliability is certain. It is supernatural guidance, the guidance available to you regardless of your situation, location or time of day or night. How do you avail yourself of this power and confidence in making decisions? First of all you must have that genuine relationship to Jesus Christ we talked about. In effect, you must be "plugged in" to the power source. This is the foundation I have been talking about. Beyond that it is merely a matter of asking for guidance and He'll provide it.

> If you want to know what God wants you to do, ask Him, and He will gladly tell you, for He is always ready to give a bountiful supply of wisdom to all who ask Him; He will not resent it. But when you ask Him, be sure that you really expect Him to tell you, for a doubtful mind will be as unsettled as a wave of the sea that is driven and tossed by the wind; and every decision you then make will be uncertain, as you turn first this way, and then that. If you don't ask with faith, don't expect the Lord to give you any solid answer (James 1:5-8, *The Living Bible*).

> The Lord, your Redeemer, the Holy One of Israel, says, I am the Lord your God, who punishes you for your own good and leads you along the paths that you should follow (Isaiah 48:17, *The Living Bible*).

The application of these promises is not complicated, but as you can see, it does have a prerequisite, beyond being "plugged in" to the power source. You must be in constant communication with Him through Bible reading and prayer, and you must ask in faith and trust in Him that the results are His will for your life (Ps. 1:2, 3; 1 John 5:14, 15). You won't hear an audible voice, nor will you feel a bolt of lightning inside you. You must put yourself in His care, trust in His ability to open and close doors for you and to place in your mind the concept of the right thing to do. Then do what seems best within that framework. He won't let you make a mistake.

You say, "That's preposterous! It just can't work that way! How can God convey the right decision to my mind even if I concede that He probably knows what I should do?" Are you forgetting that God created you and that mind of yours to begin with? And if He created it, put it all together, don't you think He would at least have the capability of planting the right decision in your mind? But then why doesn't He do this for everyone? Why is the world in such a mess? Because God didn't want a captive audience. He wants a willing audience. He doesn't want a bunch of "robots" here on earth worshiping Him. He wants people to accept Him and worship Him of their own free will. That will bring much more glory to Him than a forced worship. So he gave man a choice. And because man chose the sin route, the world is certainly in a mess and always has been since sin entered into it. But God hasn't given up yet. One day He'll shut off His offer, and then it'll be too late. But right now the offer is still open. At least it's still open to you as long as you're alive to accept it, and you don't really have any guarantee of tomorrow or next week, do you?

Let me give you just one example or illustration to help you understand how God can communicate with your mind, even without your awareness.

Man has discovered the concept of the transmission of radio waves through the atmosphere over long distances. We can even transmit pictures, along with sound, through this system (television). The technology of all this is interesting in relationship to my point here. These waves are created by a transmitter stationed in some remote spot from the receiver. The transmitter is a highly complex device which must be critically tuned for maximum power output and must also be critically tuned to a particular frequency on which it is transmitting. This frequency is so critical that you can have several transmitters within a few feet of each other pouring tremendous electrical energy into different frequencies, all without any interference either at the transmitter or at the receiving point. Basically the same thing happens at the receiving point. A radio receiver capable of tuning to hundreds or thousands of frequencies is critically adjusted to a particular frequency and the radio waves are received clearly.

A receiver can be surrounded by many powerful stations within a short distance of it and still be able to shut them out by critically tuning to a weaker station that may be thousands of miles away.

If man can discover concepts such as this and put them to work for himself, can't we at least concede that God (who created the mind of man as well as the laws of the universe on which these radios operate), can operate a similar system between His mind and the minds of men? Of course we can! So then, how do we receive these signals I am talking about? First we must have the receiver. The room in which you are sitting can be jammed with radio or television waves, but unless you have a receiver you can be completely oblivious of it. We get this receiver by accepting it as a gift from God as we receive the plan of salvation He has provided for us. Then we must plug the receiver into a power source. Thus we avail ourselves of the power of God by a close communion with Him in the reading of the Word and prayer. Then we must tune our receiver to the appointed frequency to shut out unwanted signals and interference. At times, this tuning may be very critical and difficult to adjust. But we must orient our attitude toward what God wants us to do and have the faith to believe that what He tells us will be best for us, as I pointed out previously from the epistle of James.

A good rule to help us in this critical tuning procedure is to remember the command and promise of Christ in His Sermon on the Mount, "But seek ye first the kingdom of God, and his righteousness; and all these things shall be added unto you" (Matt. 6:33).

At the risk of being misunderstood or misinterpreted, let me give you my personal formula for determining God's will in specific situations. Let me warn you, however, of two things concerning it.

1. This is not necessarily the detailed system that *you* should follow. What I have said heretofore and the Word of God should be of overriding value to the details of any "system." You may develop a system of your own and this may change from time to time.

2. If you attempt to use my system, be sure you follow my instructions implicitly, particularly the fact that *each* step is a pre-requisite to the next and that if you do not follow any step completely, *all* steps following are completely null and void.

The basic procedure is that set forth by the late A. W. Tozer in his tract, "How the Lord Leads" (Christian Publications, Incorporated, Harrisburg, Pennsylvania). I have added some final steps to it to add further practicality to its use, and to prevent its misuse.

I have given the procedure seven steps, each of which must be followed exactly to validate the next step. Do *not* start at step seven. This would be ridiculous. Some will even criticize the inclusion of step seven in the sequence. I firmly believe, however, that if the first six steps are followed honestly and completely and there is no direction apparent, then step seven is the only viable, practical alternative.

Here are the seven steps:

1. You must be "born again" into the family of God. You must have accepted Jesus Christ as your personal Savior and have established Him as the foundation for your life.

2. You must have yielded your life to His direction and

for His glory. Above all else, you must have a desire for His will in your life, regardless of whether or not it brings personal or financial success. If you can't accept His will when it brings adversity to you, for whatever reason God may have, then you have no right to seek His guidance in success. In that case, stop here, go no further until you are ready and willing to accept His will regardless of the outcome.

3. If we expect Him to guide us and communicate with us, we must keep Him "tuned in" to our mind and our daily activities through reading His Word and talking with Him daily. We can't expect advice and counsel from someone we're not on "speaking-terms" with. We talk to Him through prayer. He talks to us through His Word. The conversation must be two-way and regular.

4. There are certain things in His Word that we are commanded to do (such as "love our neighbor"). Never ask God if it's all right to do something He has already commanded us to do, just do it! Contrarily there are certain things forbidden in the Scriptures such as "vengeance" or "lying." Never ask God if it's His will to do something He has forbidden. Just don't do it!

5. Remind God that He has promised to lead you and that in this particular situation you are claiming that promise and ask Him not to permit you to make a mistake.

6. Do what seems best to you or what makes the most common sense. Don't do something illogical, unsound or unusual just because it may seem more spiritual to do so. Don't feel you must do something "odd" so it will appear to others that God is leading you. God doesn't operate that way. If you decide, based on good judgment and complete submission to His will, and your decision is wrong, then He'll let you know. He will make it clear that a particular door is closed. You won't have to guess about it.

If it's a business situation (unless God *very* plainly indicates otherwise), follow the very best sound business judgment you can obtain from the information you can gather and the tools of analysis you have available. Above all, be diligent in this gathering and analysis. Don't do a halfway job and expect God to fill in for your laziness or incompetence. In this case, too, if you are diligent and choose the best alternative according to the judgment He has given you, He won't let you make a mistake. If the choice is wrong, He'll stop you and the signals will be clear.

7. But what about the times when you can honestly say there is no *best* way to go, that good judgment still does not make clear the decision? What about the times when there are two or more alternatives that are equally sound?

If you have honestly, before God, fulfilled step six and there appears to be no *best* way (remember, step six is not a "bolt out of the blue" or a "divine revelation" — it's just using good sense). If in just using good sense you still don't have an answer you can pursue, then there is one more step that I have used on rare occasions. Do not, however, bring any potential alternatives to this step that are not good, sound judgment in themselves. This is *not* a means of "testing" the oddball, illogical or unsound routes. The alternatives inserted here must be both honoring to God and sound in business judgment.

If they qualify thusly, then you can use a type of fleece (Judg. 6:36-40) to determine the best choice. If a fleece is used to choose or not choose a single alternative (a go or no-go decision), the fleece must qualify in three ways.

   a. It must be an unusual happening (Gideon made sure by reversing the process).

   b. It must not be beneficial or rewarding in any way to you. It must be inert as it relates to you and the choice. (Gideon's fleece being wet or dry was of no material benefit to Gideon.) I have seen salary levels used as a fleece and I'm convinced that this is an abuse of the God-given procedure.

   c. Obviously, God must be involved when you use this type of approach and you must communicate your desire with regard to the fleece with Him.

I have also found another way to use a fleece in those rare instances when I have been faced with two or more viable decisions. I have assigned relative weights to them according to my very best judgment. I have then also assigned a relative weight to a "no answer" or "wait" alternative. After taking these steps, I have brought them all together, prayed about it, and then made a random selection based on the relative weights.

You may prefer some other method. The important thing is that you ask God to direct the choice. This may sound like a sacrilege to do it this way, I know. But if you have followed carefully everything I have said leading up to it, the "fleece" act in itself should not give you trouble.

The important thing is that this is an internal guidance system which "works," is practical, and does not conflict with the ethics or standards that the non-Christian world has established for us. Too often, Christians make business decisions which they attribute to God's direction, but which are obviously bad business judgment decisions. This creates a tremendous stumbling block to non-Christians and damages the witness of the Christian. I don't believe God leads us to make these kinds of decisions. He may stop us and turn us in another direction through circumstances beyond our control, but rarely does He ever ask us to make a bad business judgment decision willingly.

Everyone has an internal guidance system brought into play in the decision making process. Which kind do you have and is it reliable? You *can* have the kind I've been talking about, and it *is* reliable. How about it?

That extra something that management
experts and great leaders have never been
able to define or explain, which enables
a person to keep going even with extra drive
when everything else indicates that
he should give up.

21.

UNEXPLAINABLE,
UNDEFINABLE—MOTIVATION

The third and last of the "plus" qualities in successful
management is what I call motivation. I'm not sure that's
the right term because the term motivation itself is not
easily definable. But it deals with the "drive" or push
which certain people have that keeps them going when
you'd think that their batteries must have long since run
down. I'm certain some of this is biological. It lies in their
make-up, for they just seem to be supplied with boundless
energy. But that isn't what I'm referring to here. I'm talking about that "extra" energy or desire that makes you go
when your biological energy has run out. Some would call
it "stamina" and perhaps that is a good word to use. To
some, however, stamina would indicate more an ability
to resist and "stick it out" rather than a real aggressive position. I'm talking about an aggressive stamina. Given the
proper set of circumstances and sufficient incentive to do
so, our physical and mental system is capable of a great
deal more than we normally impose on it.

I appreciate the late J. F. Lincoln of Lincoln Electric
Company. In many of his writings he estimated that rarely
does anyone ever achieve more than fifty percent of his

potential and that most people operate on only twenty per-cent of their potential. During his lifetime he went on to prove this theory by installing an incentive system in his company. This motivation-producing philosophy increased his production several-fold and caused average factory workers to draw management level wages. We have seen this illustrated in the realm of physical strength. People faced with an emergency situation have been known to perform feats of strength normally impossible. Several years ago, one of our popular national weekly magazines carried a story about a 130-pound navy lieutenant. During the devastating fire aboard the U.S.S. *Forrestal* off Viet Nam, he picked up a 250-pound bomb and heaved it overboard when it threatened to explode in the midst of a group of men. The emergency had given him physical strength considerably beyond that normally available to him. In a similar way J. F. Lincoln provided a set of circumstances in his factory which caused his people to call on and de-velop mental and physical resources that allowed them to double or triple their former performance.

One caution here might be in order when one deals with other people along these lines. You can't create motiva-tion in other people. You can create a set of circumstances that might lead to motivation, but the desire for it and the creation of it must come from within the individual. Na-turally he might consider the circumstances you have pro-vided him in a different light than you do. So my discus-sion here is centered primarily on personal motivation, not on how to motivate others.

Another phenomenon often develops. We place imagin-ary limitations on ourselves and then these imaginary limi-tations become very real and actual physical limitations. This is because our mind has told our body it can't be done and therefore it really can't be done. Let me illustrate again. For years in track and field athletic competition, the four-minute mile was considered beyond man's physical capabilities. Thousands of athletes regularly attempted to break this limitation but it just couldn't be done. Then one day an athlete, who refused to believe it couldn't be done, did it. But the amazing thing is not what he did. It is what other athletes were able to do after this psychological barrier had been removed. Within five years after that, the four-minute mile barrier had been broken by twenty-one different runners — fifty different times! And within fifteen years 107 runners had broken the record 320 different times! The four-minute mile was considered beyond human capacity just a few years before.

I am reminded of another rather stunning example of that "extra-something" which makes the difference between success and failure. Recently I read an article on the twenty-fifth anniversary of the invasion of France in World War Two. Here was a situation involving one of the largest and most complex organizations in history. Years of preparation had gone into training the thousands of men involved. The leadership was the very best the free world could provide. Several nations were coordinated in the drive. The greatest military strategy and genius of history planned the invasion. The equipment and fire power was unlike anything ever amassed before. Yet Cornelius Ryan, author of *The Longest Day,* learned (after his book was published) that the invasion of Normandy Beach almost failed.

Even with the greatest combination of people, planning, equipment, dedication and sacrifice the Allies could muster, at noon that day they seemed doomed to failure. Back in England, a communique was being prepared announcing the failure of the attack. If it had failed, it was estimated eighteen more months would be required to put together another invasion. During that time the Nazis might have sued for peace and we might have given in to some of their terms. Or we might have met the Russians at the French border instead of in Germany. The entire course of world affairs would probably have been altered.

But the invasion didn't fail. What got it going after being stalled on the beach for hours with everyone, including the generals, ready to give up?

Ryan said his explanation sounded corny and unprofessional but was apparently true. "Finally guys started just getting tired of being hit and not moving. A sergeant kicked someone in the pants. Another man said he preferred getting killed going up the beach rather than sitting on it . . . that's the way it was, though. There's no better explanation."

Once the Americans had left the beaches and reached the hedgerows and meadows beyond, "the chances were infinitely smaller for them to be driven back," Ryan said.

While this example may be a little crude, it is a significant, history-changing example of that "extra-something" that spells the difference.

I think maybe I have a "hang-up" in this area because I personally do not have that natural abounding energy and drive I often see in others. My enthusiasm has to be pumped up and I guess it bothered me over the years to see my dad go at a pace nearly twice my capacity, even though he was nearly forty years older than I. For this reason particularly I have given a great deal of study to this matter of motivation and drive. I wanted to find out how I could develop my own. It certainly isn't easy to do, I can tell you that. But it can be done with the proper goals in life and the sustaining power available from God. I'm not saying that enthusiasm can't be pumped up without God's help but only a few people, those who are naturally so endowed, can do it. Part of the reason is that, without Christ, there is nothing beyond the fleeting moments of this life here on earth. With this limited outlook it becomes difficult to motivate oneself. It is easier to relax and be lazy, when all that you are really doing is amassing a few dollars to leave to someone else. Christians, on the other hand, have eternity to look forward to and the rewards God has promised His faithful stewards. Thus they can't really lose what they have gained if they are operating within His plan for their lives.

Success in the field of management, getting the job done through people, is pretty much limited as a whole to those

few individuals who either naturally or artificially have
that extra drive. This is the motivation and stamina that
keeps them going when everyone else peters out. In many
ways it is an unexplainable and undefinable quality but
it is there. If you don't have it, it is still available to you,
but you must have a strong desire for it. This desire comes
most easily if you have real purpose in your life, if you
are serving the Lord and fulfilling His plan for your life.
It is only necessary to have your foundation in Christ. You
must be plugged in to the power of God and then come
to a full realization of what that power can really do for
you.

> I pray that your hearts will be flooded with light so that
> you can see something of the future He has called you to
> share. . . . I pray that you will begin to understand how
> incredibly great His power is to help those who believe in
> Him . . . (Ephesians 1:18, 19, *The Living Bible*).

With this light and this power, you, too, can have that
extra drive and motivation in your life, that extra dimension
so vital in *Management "Plus"* so essential to a successful
career.

CONCLUSION

By now you are undoubtedly convinced (or should be) that this is not a rule book, not a book of "pat" answers in the management field. Rather it is a book of dynamics with a code to live by as well as some concepts of management which may not have been called to your attention previously. While these are not "rules" per se, they can be effective guides to a more successful career — particularly when the concepts of the "plus" are allowed to take effect in your career.

While management is, in many ways, a science, and much of it can be relegated to do's and don't's and rules to follow, it is also an art. People through whom the job must get done do not always lend themselves so easily to such scientific analysis. Thus this book is, as it was intended to be, a living and vital approach to the age-old problems confronting the person who must manage others.

Because management is not a science in the strict sense of the word, it cannot be learned from a textbook. If you were a genius and could memorize this entire book word for word, and if you also had the time and the ability to choose the right concept for each situation and apply it properly, you still would not be a good manager. Management must be lived and practiced, not just learned. In the same vein, real Christianity cannot result from mere head knowledge. It must be a living vital experience. Management, like Christianity, must be exercised in a dynamic setting where experience and judgment is exercised. And within certain bounds a great deal of freedom and latitude may be utilized. How much better is this freedom than being confined within the constrictions or the rules set forth in this book.

For example, think of a person who is a great mathematician, physicist and engineer and knows all of the laws of motion, balance, strength, leverage, gravity, etc. If he had never ridden a bicycle, however, he would surely take a bad fall the first time he tried! It would undoubtedly be helpful for him to have this head knowledge, but experience and freedom to use these facts without even giving serious thought to them is what would make him a good bicycle rider.

The same is true of a skilled typist, an accounting machine operator, an automobile racer, or a photographer handling a complex camera. The rules must all be obeyed within bounds, certainly, or disaster will result. But the rules must be so well in mind through experience and feel that they are put into action with complete freedom, almost instinctively.

This, then, is the real manager or leader. He is the one who can lead and manage and work through people with complete freedom from the constriction of rules — and yet not violate any of the basic concepts in so doing.

Likewise, the Christian who is living close to God and is constantly in His Word, is "not entangled again with the yoke of bondage," but is "in the liberty wherewith Christ hath made us free" (Gal. 5:1). Freedom here does not mean license. Just as the manager must be guided by his experience and concepts, the Christian is also "free, not using your liberty for a cloak of maliciousness, but as the servants of God" (1 Pet. 2:16).

Thus a Christian has freedom rather than being entangled with rules and laws. But this freedom (like the freedom we have in driving a car) is a controlled freedom, in this case controlled by our walk with God and the light of His love.

Let me conclude with what I feel is a sad commentary on so many Christians in business today. With the concepts set forth in the Scriptures (and all of the qualities in this book can be backed up by sound scriptural illustrations), the Christian, working and managing in the business arena, can unquestionably be a better prepared and able manager than any who are without the power of God in their lives. And yet, we see so few businessmen who are really "out and out" for Christ and following these concepts.

If you know Christ as your Savior and will follow the guidelines established here, availing yourself of His power, you, yourself, can be a better manager than anyone (and I do mean *anyone*) who does not know Christ and does not have His power available to him. Notice I said, "You *can be.*" Whether you *will be* or not is up to you.

Christian in business, whether you have been a Christian for thirty minutes or thirty years, *I dare you* to apply these concepts in your business and in your everyday life and accept the challenge of God in Malachi 3:10 that He will "Open you the windows of heaven and pour you out a blessing that there shall not be room enough to receive it."

How about it? I DARE YOU!